TRUE TALES
of
TEXAS

The Tejas had the right idea. (*See page 277*)

TRUE TALES OF TEXAS

BY

Bertha Mae Cox

Dallas Public Schools

ILLUSTRATED BY

Lura Ann Taylor Hedrick

A Facsimile Reproduction of the Original

Hendrick-Long Publishing Co.

HOUSTON - TEXAS

Cox, Bertha Mae,
True tales of Texas.

Reprint. Originally published: Dallas : Turner Co., 1949.
Includes index.
Summary: A collection of tales about people and events in Texas history arranged in chronological order from the sixteenth century to the present day.
1. Texas–History–Juvenile literature. [1. Texas–History] I. Hedrick, Lura Ann Taylor, ill. II. Title.
F386.3.C68 1987 976.4 87-12091
ISBN 0-937460-77-X (pb.)
ISBN 0-937460-28-1 (cb.)
Hendrick-Long Publishing Co.
Houston, Texas

Dedicated to

BETTY JO CANNON

for whom

some of these stories

were first told

INTRODUCTION

The traditional, folk-way method of transmitting history has long been simply the telling of stories or tales. Many years of working with boys and girls has made me a fervent advocate of this approach to history.

True Tales of Texas was designed for reading aloud and re-telling at story time. The rhythm —and I hope, the beauty of speech—will be evident only in oral reading.

I trust that the young readers of this book will develop an appreciation of what history really means and will know some of our sources for learning it.

The plan of the book is simple. The poem, taken from *Dreamers on Horseback* by Karle Wilson Baker, gives an over-all picture of the past and present in our state and brings a vision of the courage and strength of its builders. The stories are a collection of the most dramatic persons and events in the history of our state. They are arranged in chronological order, beginning with Cabeza de Vaca about 1528 and ending with the present time.

Dates are given by comparison, rather than by naming a figure that is often meaningless to a child. For instance, terms like these are used: almost three hundred years ago, two years after the Battle of San Jacinto, a century ago.

The vocabulary has been kept easy and simple, and carefully tested by classroom use. I have made no effort to check this vocabulary against a standardized word list. Every good, experienced teacher knows the *way* words are used is as important as *what* words are used. By actual testing with children, and re-writing the parts they did not readily grasp, I am sure these ideas are clothed in words the children can readily understand.

The sentences are short. Instead of a long complex sentence, I have used a series of short sentences, often keeping the continuity by beginning the last sentence with *and*. Such a plan makes it easy to get the thought from the printed page.

The chapters on Texas Towns and Texas Counties are in keeping with the trend to combine the study of geography and history. The two are inseparably united. Places are often named for characters of history; and we have only half the picture unless we know both *what* happened and *where* the event occurred.

The repetition of basal facts is not by accident. Learning comes by much patient re-telling.

The illustrator of *True Tales of Texas* has won various honors and recognition of her ability as an artist. She, too, is a teacher. She has worked closely with children in planning and creating the pictures. We knew she had succeeded in interpreting the child's point of view when a little boy made the following comment. He had just looked at the illustration for the story about Cynthia Ann Parker and said, "That is the way I thought they looked. I just knew the Chief would pass by the grapevine swing."

I have endeavored to make the manner of storytelling vivid and colorful, warm, and blessed with the human touch. Many times I have told a historical fact by putting it in conversation in the first person. It is my earnest desire that the children who read this book will find it an experience of sheer joy.

I believe that every book, without being didactic, should be a source for character education. I've tried to make it clear that our early heroes are not honored because they happened to live long ago but for qualities of character.

Friendliness and fairness for all peoples of the world are sought after by all thoughtful leaders. I've tried to develop appreciation for and understanding of all groups and nationalities throughout the book and have emphasized this thought in the last chapter.

Last, and most important, there is no similar material on our bookshelves. Most of our school books are written in the East. From the third grade up the children read stories of our national heroes. This builds a background for American History. Boys and girls have no such preparation for Texas History. As a result, they sometimes think this vital and dramatic subject hard and uninteresting.

True Tales of Texas is especially planned to precede and to prepare for the study of Texas History.

BERTHA MAE COX

Sept. 1, 1949
Dallas, Texas

To the Boys and Girls:

Do you enjoy hearing your grandfather tell of things that happened when he was a boy? Have you ever gathered around the fireside on a chilly winter evening and heard someone tell of events that occurred on the very spot when the Indians lived here? Or, have you ever gone camping, and in the drowsy twilight listened to tales of treasure buried by the Spanish somewhere in that region, perhaps at your very campsite? When you listened to these tales of long ago, did you feel brave and strong? Did you think that had you been here then you would not have been afraid?

Then perhaps you would like to hear about a little girl. Her father knew the nicest stories and was seldom too busy to tell them. When he came home in the evening this little girl would run to meet him. Together they would feed the horse, and hurry in to eat the supper which her mother had ready. And then it was story time!

As the little girl grew older she worked hard in the afternoons to get her lessons—arithmetic, geography, and history; for if she played too long the lessons would have to be studied at night, leaving no time for stories.

And such wonderful stories they were! About how the Indians lived in Texas, about Austin, and Houston, and a little girl named Cynthia Ann. He told about the early churches and the early schools, and of how their town and county got its name.

This little girl called the book *history* and what her father told her *stories* and *tales.* It was not until years later that she learned they were the finest kind of history in all the world.

I know, because I was once that funny little girl.

THE AUTHOR

Lura Ann Taylor

SIX FLAGS OF TEXAS

The Spanish flag first waved over our land. Cabeza de Vaca, a Spaniard, was the first white man to walk on Texas soil. Not long after him came De Soto, and Coronado, who staked the plains of the Panhandle. We still call them the Staked Plains.

La Salle planted the French flag in Texas. He was here only a few years, but these brave Frenchmen left many things to remind us of their colony. The first wedding in Texas was held in La Salle's colony.

When Mexico won its independence from Spain, Texas became a part of Mexico and was under the Mexican flag.

But Texas was under the Mexican flag only fifteen years. At San Jacinto, April 21, 1836, brave Texan soldiers, under the command of Sam Houston, won freedom for our land.

For ten years Texas was a republic—a free nation. The flag was the Lone Star flag. When Texas became a state in the United States, the lone star flag was kept as the state flag.

Then came the sad days of the War between the States. Texas was in the South, so was under the flag of the Southern Confederacy. We now know that both sides were a little right and a little wrong, so we are glad to forget our family quarrel.

Our national flag now is Old Glory, the flag of the United States of America. We are proud of this flag and of all that it stands for.

> "Long may it wave,
> O'er the land of the free
> And the home of the brave."

CONTENTS

Lura

TRUE TALES
of
TEXAS

SONG OF THE FORERUNNERS

from

DREAMERS ON HORSEBACK

by

KARLE WILSON BAKER *

(Arranged for Choral Reading)

Boys:

The men who made Texas
Rode west with dazzled eyes
On the hot trail of the Future,
To take her by surprise:

They were dreamers on horseback,
Dreamers with strong hands,
Trailing the golden Lion
Who couches in far lands:

Old men and young men, little men and tall,
Bad men and good men—but strong men, all.

Girls:

The women who bore Texas
Could see beyond the sun:
They sat on cabin doorsteps
When the long day was done,

And they crooned to lusty babies,
But their look was far away—
For they gazed straight through the sunset
To the unborn day.

Stern women, laughing women, women stout or small,
Bronzed women, broken women—brave women, all.

Boys:

The men who made Texas
Laughed at fate and doom—
Dreamers on horseback,
Men who needed room;

Girls:

And the women in young Texas,
Hanging homespun clothes to dry,
Loved a prairie for a dooryard,
For meeting-house, the sky—

All:

Wide visions and wide spaces, man and land were large of lung:
Texas knew not cheap and easy, slack and small, when she was young!

Boys:

But the men who made Texas
Left their work half-done—
For nothing stands full-finished
Beneath the spinning sun;

Girls:

And the women who dreamed Texas
Had much work to do
When they lay down for their last sleep
In a land still new;

All:

And a yet-unbuilded Texas, cloud-paved and glimmering,
Burns yet before the eyes of us, who toil and dream and sing.

SOMETHING TO THINK ABOUT

1. Who are the forerunners of Texas?

2. Name some things we enjoy today that were given us by our forefathers.

3. Has all the work of building a great state and nation been completed? Is there anything you can do?

4. Memorize this poem and give it as a choral reading on an assembly program.

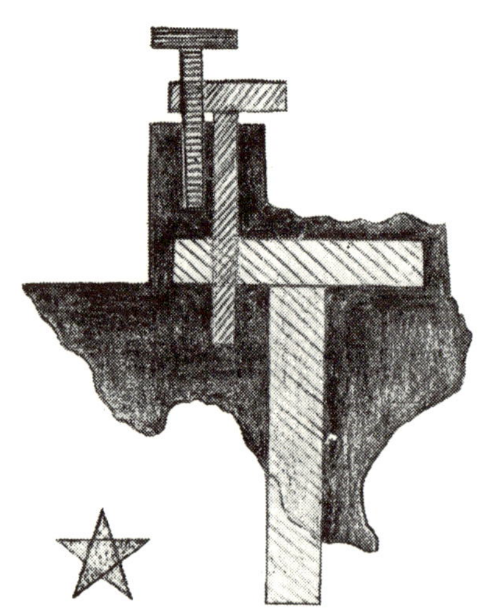

THE FIRST TELLER OF TALL TALES

Christopher Columbus, as everyone knows, was sailing under the Spanish flag when he discovered America. He claimed all the land for Spain. No one even imagined how much land there was in the New World. How surprised Columbus would have been had anyone told him!

About twenty-five years after the discovery voyage of Christopher Columbus, the King of Spain sent out an exploring party. There were five ships and six hundred men.

"Go to this new land," said the King to the commander. "Keep a record of all you see. Make a map of the country. Then come back and tell me all about it."

They sailed first to the islands of the West Indies. Then they went to Florida. Here they contracted malaria and many of them died. Too, the Indians were unfriendly. Between the mosquitoes and wild Indians, the king's explorers were having a very bad time. So they set out to find a Spanish settlement which is now Mexico City.

"It can't be far away," they said.

Little did they know that about fifteen hundred long miles lay between them and their goal.

They followed the coastline around to the place we now know as Galveston. There was a storm and the boats were separated and wrecked. Four survivors were washed ashore on Galveston Island.

These Spaniards called it Malhado (mäl-hä′dō), or the Island of Bad Luck.

These men were Cebeza de Vaca (kä bā′ sä dā vä kä), Dorantes (dō-rän′tās), Castillo (cäs tēl′-yō), and Esteban (ās tā′bän). The first three were Spanish explorers. Esteban was the negro slave of Dorantes.

Poor men, they were in a sad plight. They had no food. They had lost their clothing. And it was winter. A cold rain was falling, freezing as it fell.

The Karankawa (kă-răng′kä-wä) Indians lived near the coast. They were the largest of

Everyone wanted to know about this strange new world.

all the Texas Indians. These brown giants were also very fierce and warlike.

But the pitiful condition of these men aroused the sympathy of even the savages. Too, the Indians feared these strange men. They had never seen a man with white skin before. Nor had they ever seen anyone with black skin. The Indians probably were as amazed as you would be if, tomorrow morning, on your way to school, you met three men with blue skin and one with green!

The Indians shared with them their scanty food of roots and berries. Since the men were too weak to walk, the Indians carried them on their backs. Every few miles, they stopped, built a fire, and put these chilled men beside it to warm.

Slowly the men recovered. Cabeza de Vaca began to keep notes of what they saw and did. It was not an easy thing to do. He had no calendar, so he could know the time only by the seasons, carefully recording four seasons as one year. He wrote his notes on pieces of bark or anything else he could use. Sometimes a thorn served as his pencil.

The Indians, whose religion was the worship of the gods of nature and many beliefs of superstition, called the white men the Children of the Sun. Esteban was worshiped by some of the tribes. The Indians said that surely these men whose appearance was so unusual must possess extraordinary powers. They made Cabeza de Vaca, who was leader of the four by common consent, a medicine man. He protested that he knew nothing about treating diseases. But they told him plainly that he must do something to pay for his food; and if he did not want himself and his companions killed to get busy at once curing all the sick members of the tribe! And while he was about it, they said, he should see that the Spirit of the Four Winds brought them good luck, too!

Poor Cabeza de Vaca! His was not an easy task. And yet, he dared not try, for their very lives were at stake. Castillo's father was a doctor in Spain. He had learned a few things by observation. He told his companion all he knew. The Spaniards knew about cleanliness, food, and the general rules of health. Their knowledge was very much like what you study in classes on Health. But the savage Indians did not know even these simple things.

We do not know who Cabeza de Vaca's first patient was. It might have been a boy or a girl about your age. We do know something of the treatment, for Cabeza de Vaca made note of it in his journal.

The Indian medicine men danced round and round the sick person, yelling wildly all the time. They took turns, and kept this up day and night. They did this, they said, to frighten away the evil spirits which had caused the illness.

Though Cabeza de Vaca made motions over the patient (he did that only to please the Indians), he did it quietly. He gave the sick Indian some light, nourishing food. Perhaps he gave him a warm bath and made the bed more comfortable. All night he sat there, making weird motions. The patient slept. Next morning he felt much better.

"The White Man has magic power," said the Indians. "He knows all dark secrets."

Soon other tribes heard that Cabeza de Vaca was the best medicine man in the whole country. They, too, brought their sick ror him to heal.

It is said that Cabeza de Vaca performed the first surgical operation in Texas. It happened like this.

An Indian was brought to him with an arrowhead deeply imbedded near the heart. Cabeza de Vaca was afraid to attempt to remove the arrowhead. But he knew the Indians would kill him if he did not try. And yet, he also knew they would surely kill him if he came too near the heart and the Indian died. He had only a pocket knife, and Spanish moss for dressing. When the Indians began their prayerful chant, Cabeza de Vaca wrote that he prayed more earnestly than he ever had before in all his life. He removed the arrowhead. The Indian lived.

Now the Indians' admiration was greater than ever. They gave him the choicest food and the best bed. Even the chief obeyed his every command.

While we know that Cabeza de Vaca did sometimes exaggerate, he wrote in his journal that in one week they brought as many as three thousand sick Indians to him. No wonder he wanted to escape and go to Mexico.

There were many tribes of Indians in Texas. They were constantly at war, so that it was very difficult for those in one area to get what they needed from another area. Cabeza de Vaca was shrewd enough to see this. He was granted privileges which they did not have. As a medicine man, he went from tribe to tribe. So he began trading between the tribes. Those who lived many miles from the coast were glad to get shells for cutting and making into beads. In exchange he carried back to the shore Indians ochre, which they used to color their bodies, and deer sinews for bows. He made many friends among the Indians in this way. Besides, as a merchant he was sent on long trips. In this way he learned much about the country and how the Indians lived. Since Cabeza de Vaca kept notes of all these things, we know something of how the Indians of that day lived.

Most of the Indians killed deer and caught fish. Prickly pears were a great delicacy. When they were in season, the Indians who lived on the shore traveled many miles that they might eat them. Some of the tribes were intelligent enough to dry the pears and pack them away like dried figs to be saved until needed. Mesquite beans were an important food, too.

Very few of the Indians knew how to make pottery. The less intelligent tribes dug holes in the ground and put into them whatever food they had.

Gourds grew wild. The Indians scooped out the seeds and used them very much as we do today. Although these vessels could not be set on the fire, the Indians cooked in them. They put water and the food to be cooked into the gourds. Then they heated rocks, which were put into the gourds. In this way the food was cooked.

At that time there were no horses here. Some years later the Spaniards brought horses to our country. Some of them got loose and could not be caught. They became wild horses which we call mustangs (mŭs′tăngs).

But the Indians Cabeza de Vaca knew had never seen a horse. A few tribes had no bows and arrows. How would you kill a deer if you had neither bow and arrow nor a horse? One tribe had an answer to that question. They had men who could run so long and so fast that they could follow a deer until it was tired down, then catch it, and kill it.

The Indians were very clever in warfare. They fought bending low on the ground or from behind trees. When they were being shot at, they would leap about very fast to avoid the arrows.

Cabeza de Vaca tells us about the homes of the Indians, too. The Tejas (tā′häs) Indians, who planted gardens and, after a manner, had permanent homes, lived in rude houses built of small logs plastered with mud. The tribes that moved about had tepees of skins.

These Spanish explorers were the first Europeans to see the American buffalo.

For about eight years these four men lived in Texas. All of this time Cabeza de Vaca was making notes. He made a map of Texas. They walked all the way across the state, from Galveston Island to El Paso. From there they managed to escape and made their way to a Spanish settlement in Mexico.

When Cabeza de Vaca, Dorantes, Castillo, and Esteban finally arrived in Mexico, the Governor had a great celebration in their honor. All the people had given them up as dead. They had undergone such hardships that they had to rest several months before starting back to Spain. They got back home just ten years from the time they left.

The King of Spain sent for them to come to the palace. He wanted to know about this strange New World. Every one else did, too. Of the group, Cabeza de Vaca was the most sought after. Perhaps he was the most interesting storyteller. Certainly it was he who had the written record of their adventures.

At once Cabeza de Vaca became the hero of his time in Spain. Everywhere he went, he was asked over and over again to tell of his adventures. There was no one to contradict him. So each time he told his story it became bigger and bigger. As we read his account today, we know that it contained gross exaggerations. Much of his journal is true. But some is a tall tale. So we may call Cabeza de Vaca the first teller of tall tales.

Cabeza de Vaca told them of seven great cities, of which the Indians told him but which he did not claim to have seen, where the streets were paved with gold. Other people who heard the story of the explorers added exaggerations of their own. Silver and gold were all over the ground, they said.

Everyone became very excited. Many explorers wanted to cross the ocean and obtain these riches. Several expeditions were sent out. Two of these expeditions, those of De Soto and Coronado, came into Texas.

And so Texas was explored many years earlier by the Spaniards because Cabeza de Vaca was a teller of tall tales.

TALL TALES BY YOUNG TEXANS

Do you ever "play-like"? Of course you do!
Pretend you are Cabeza de Vaca telling his story

at the Spanish court. Make up the very best story you can. Tell your story to your classmates.

Perhaps you would like to take the part of some other character in this story.

I think you will have fun making up your stories!

STORY OF LA SALLE

Many years ago there lived in Rouen, France a boy named Robert Cavelier. He was the youngest son of a wealthy merchant. Everyone said that Robert was a bright boy and that he was very handsome. His parents wanted him to have a good education. Almost all the schools at that time were conducted by the church. They were called monastery schools. It was to one of these that young Robert was sent. When he graduated, his teachers gave him a certificate of good character and excellent record in all his studies.

His teachers, who were priests, said, "Robert is one of the best students we have ever had in our school. He understands all that we teach him about the church. He may become a priest."

His mother said, "I think our youngest son, Robert, has a very bright future. He may become a priest. That would please me very much." And his father agreed.

But Robert was making other plans. He listened to the wonderful stories of the New World. Both Spaniards and Frenchmen were seeking fortunes there, and he heard reports of their travels. The young man's father and uncle had business interests in Canada. His older brother was a missionary there. So at the age of twenty-three Robert Cavelier set sail for this wonderful land beyond the sea.

Shortly after his arrival in Canada, he was given a large grant of land by the French king. He improved his land, studied Indian languages and customs, and explored the country round about. For his splendid service to his country in claiming the land for France, the king made him a noble and bestowed upon him a title. His full name now was Monsieur Robert Cavelier Sieur de la Salle. He is remembered in history as La Salle (lȧ säl) and that is what we shall call him in this story.

One winter some Indians came to La Salle's trading post. They told him of a great river that flowed into an ocean where big ships sailed. They called it the "Father of Waters."

La Salle at once began making preparations

"This is a great occasion," said La Salle.

for exploring this river. When spring came, La Salle's party started out. As they moved southward, the land became greener and the flowers more colorful. La Salle loved this beautiful land. When they reached the mouth of the long Mississippi River, he stood on the spot where New Orleans now stands, and said, "Some day there will be a great city here. I should like that city to be a French city. I claim all the land drained by this river for France."

At once he started back to Canada, where he got on a boat sailing for France. La Salle had hardly greeted his family before he was off again to Paris, to tell the king of this lovely land and his plans for establishing a settlement.

The plan found favor with the king. He fitted out four ships, one of which, the *Belle,* was a personal gift from the king to La Salle. They were loaded with all kinds of supplies for the settlers—food, clothing, furniture, lumber, boats, guns, and cannons. They also brought goods to trade with the Indians. About three hundred people were on board. There were soldiers, families, doctors, and seven priests, one of whom was La Salle's own brother. There was a historian, too, and it is because he kept a record from day to day that we now know about what happened so long ago.

The expedition had been carefully planned and lavishly provided for. There was just one thing wrong—some of the people.

You know the kind of man La Salle was. Many others were as brave and good as he. But while many adventurers had come across the sea, it was something new for families to make a home here. There were many dangers. Few people wanted to come. So, in order to get enough settlers, La Salle took all who said they were willing to come. Some of them were lazy, and a few were criminals.

They set sail in August. It was not a pleasant voyage. The commander of the ships quarreled constantly with La Salle. They sailed too far south, and so missed the mouth of the Mississippi. At last they found an inlet which La Salle believed to be the western mouth of the river he was searching for, and he gave orders to land.

But La Salle was many miles from the "Father of Waters." They landed at Matagorda Bay in Texas. And thus it happened that La Salle made the second settlement in Texas, about one hundred and fifty years after Cabeza de Vaca had landed on our shores. [Ysleta (ēs-lā′tȧ), at El Paso, was settled two years before by the Spaniards.]

The commander of the ships was in an ugly temper the day they landed. He wrecked one of the ships, some thought purposely. Imagine how La Salle and the settlers felt as they saw their precious supplies floating out to sea.

But even with these misfortunes, the people were happy as they landed. It was October. And at Matagorda Bay that means warm, sunny days. Green leaves were still on the trees. The children, and even the grown-ups, wanted to run on the sandy beach. But La Salle knew of savage Indian ways, and commanded the people to stay close together.

At first they camped on Matagorda Island, where the lighthouse now stands. But the fort was built on higher ground, beside a small river. Many buffaloes came to this river to drink. La Salle named the stream Lavaca, or Cow River. We still call the river by the name which La Salle gave it so many years ago.

Building the fort was a very difficult task. They salvaged some lumber from the wrecked ship. There was no nearby timber on this prairie. Trees were cut down several miles away. They had no horses or oxen, so the men themselves dragged the logs to the site of the fort. There was not a single good carpenter in the settlement. La Salle himself had to draw the plans and mark each log for its place. Too, the Indians proved very bad neighbors. By day one never knew when an arrow would come whizzing from some hidden place. And at night, these Indians, who could howl like wolves, terrified the people with weird sounds.

As if they didn't have enough trouble already, the contrary commander of the ships announced that he was sailing back to France with the biggest and best ship.

"Be sure that you give us time to unload the ship," said La Salle.

But the next day, when only the eight cannons had been unloaded, the commander put out to sea. On board were about half the soldiers, many of their supplies—and all the cannon balls!

At last the fortress was completed. There was one large building, divided into rooms as needed. Underneath was a cellar, where the ammunition and other supplies were stored. There was a small chapel, too. Around it all was a high palisade. There were loopholes through which the French settlers could shoot at their enemy. A cannon was mounted at each corner, and was loaded with bags of bullets.

La Salle called the people together. One of the priests spoke to them.

"You have had many hardships. And yet, is it not by God's loving kindness that we who stand here have been spared? Let us gather in the chapel tomorrow for a service of thanksgiving and praise."

The people dressed as carefully as they could for the occasion. First of all, La Salle placed the flag of France above the fort. Its folds loosened in the soft summer breeze.

"I, Robert Cavelier Sieur de la Salle, name this fort St. Louis in honor of the King of France."

The people cheered.

Then they went into the chapel, where they sang a hymn and knelt in prayer.

Since his people were comfortably housed, La Salle began preparations for searching for the Mississippi River. It can't be far, he thought. He and his party traveled as far as the Trinity River. There they met the friendly Cenis Indians, part of the Tejas Confederacy.

La Salle became very ill, probably from malaria. The friendly Indians cared for him. And when the Frenchmen left to return to Fort St. Louis, the Cenis Chief gave them horses.

This was a very valuable gift. Just imagine what it would be like to walk from Dallas to Matagorda Bay, especially if one were just up from a long illness.

As these weary explorers neared Fort St. Louis, they heard music and laughter. A young couple had just been married in the little chapel. The wedding party welcomed the chief and his men with joyous shouts.

"This is a great occasion," said La Salle, as he bowed low before the bride.

And truly it was, for it was the first European wedding on Texas soil.

Then it was Christmas again. We can only wonder what Petit Noel brought the children. No doubt they missed the mechanical toys and beautiful dolls of their homeland. We may be very sure that they had homemade cakes and candy and something special for dinner. Perhaps the children made a *crêche* (krāsh). More than likely they all went to the little chapel in observance of the Holy Infant's Birthday.

About the middle of January La Salle appeared in the open square dressed for traveling. The people listened quietly as he spoke.

"You have been very brave. You have seen our number dwindle day by day. I *must* find the Mississippi and get help. We have only forty men left. I want twenty men to stay here to protect the fort, and twenty men to go with me."

Not a word was spoken as, one by one, La Salle chose the men to go with him.

"I want my brother, the priest, to go with me.

"I choose my nephews, Moranget (mō rän′-nyā) and his younger brother.

"We shall need a doctor, another priest, Nika (nē′kä), my faithful Indian guide, and Joutel (zhoo tel′), the historian."

The twenty men were chosen, and they started across the prairie. Buffaloes were plentiful, so they had no lack of meat. When the cold winter rains fell, the men made a small hut from the tall prairie grass. In this shelter they were able to stay fairly dry until the skies cleared, when they resumed traveling.

They had great difficulty in crossing the Brazos River, one of the swiftest streams in the state. They crossed on a raft. Two men refused to cross over, so swift was the current. But when they saw the others marching away on the opposite bank, they begged them to wait. At once these two began to fell trees, from which they made another raft, and crossed the swirling river.

Farther on in their travels one of the men killed a buffalo. He sent word for two other men to come help them carry the meat to camp. La Salle sent Moranget, (mō rän′nyā), his nephew, and another man.

Moranget and one of the men quarreled; and La Salle's nephew and the faithful Nika were murdered as they slept.

The murderers were frightened lest La Salle render them their just punishment.

So one wicked deed led to another. These men made their plot to kill La Salle.

For three days La Salle waited. He seemed troubled. No doubt he knew the character of these men. He gave an Indian a hatchet as payment for guiding them through the woods. He would allow only the priest to go with him and the guide.

As they walked, La Salle talked of God's love and grace. He hoped the young man was safe, he said.

They neared the camp and La Salle heard

voices. He ran toward them, calling, "Is my nephew safe?"

A gun was fired. La Salle fell, dying. This was March 19, 1687.

Today we still remember and honor brave La Salle. On or near the spot where La Salle was murdered is the town of Navasota. Here there stands a monument to the first Frenchman to come to Texas. It was through the work of La Salle that France claimed Texas, and raised the French flag over the land.

As for the rest of the men in La Salle's exploring party, theirs was a sad fate. Some of them quarreled and killed each other. Some were killed by Indians. Others died from hunger and exposure. Six men finally did reach the Mississippi River and the French settlement on the banks of the Illinois River. One of these men was Joutel, the historian. And that is how we know today of the fate of good La Salle.

What became of those left at Fort St. Louis? The Spanish tell us that.

News reached the king of Spain that there was a French settlement on the land he had claimed because of Cabeza de Vaca's travels. He ordered that an expedition be sent at once to find it. In all, eight expeditions went through Texas—searching, searching for the French fort. At last they found it.

The fort was entirely deserted. On all sides were signs of an Indian attack. But no one was there to tell what had happened. The broken guns and torn pages from French books silently told the sad story.

Some say that La Salle's life was a failure. But this is not true, for Texas today is La Salle's dream come true.

WHO?

Who planted the French flag on Texas soil?

Where was La Salle's colony? Find it on the map.

Where was the first wedding (other than the Indians) held in Texas?

Where is the statue of La Salle?

QUEEN OF THE MISSIONS

With the soldiers sent to look for La Salle's colony was a Spanish priest. He met some of the good Tejas (tā'häs) Indians, and promised to come back and build a mission for them.

Several missions were built in East Texas. They were made of pine logs, rotted away years ago.

In all about twenty-five missions were founded in Texas. Five of these were in San Antonio. They were built of stone, and are standing today. The largest and most beautiful of all the missions is Mission San Jose (sän hō sā'). An old record of the church says that, judged by strength of construction and beauty of plan, it is the finest mission in the whole Southwest. In the same letter the priest calls San Jose the Queen of the Missions.

Today, Mission San Jose, about two miles

Even the children helped.

south of San Antonio, is generally called the Queen of the Missions.

San Jose, like all the Spanish missions, had four parts: the fort with the soldiers, the civilians with their families, the converted Indians, and the church, with living quarters for the priests nearby.

One morning, more than two hundred years ago, a long procession moved from the little village of San Antonio, southward, along the San Antonio River.

Leading the procession was a Spanish priest, Father Margil (mär hēl′), one of the Franciscan fathers. He carried aloft a large wooden cross. On either side of him walked a priest. Behind were other priests and altar-boys.

Next in the procession came the Spanish soldiers, on horseback. Their bright uniforms were gay in the early morning sunshine. They carried a large Spanish flag, which waved gently in the soft breeze.

The townspeople of San Antonio followed the soldiers. Many of them had been born in Mexico, rather than Spain, and already they were sometimes called Mexicans.

Then, as proud and as straight as the king's soldiers, stalked the converted Indians. In honor of the occasion, they wore their feathered head-dresses and brightest blankets. Last of all came the Indian squaws and Indian children.

The site for the mission had been selected several days before. The Franciscan Father led them toward it now.

Not far from where they crossed the San Antonio River, on a gently rolling hill, the priest stopped and raised his hand. He started a church hymn, and the others along the strange procession began to sing, too. Thus they came, singing, to the place where San Jose was to stand.

The space was marked off, 660 feet square. Perhaps they drew the line on the ground with the point of one of the soldiers' swords. The corner-stone was set in place. Prayers were said, and the assembly dismissed.

On that day in 1720 they began the building of San Jose. It was not finished until more than sixty years later.

Everybody worked with a will—soldiers, priests, and Indians. Even the Indian and Mexican children helped, bringing sand and water. Father Margil moved among the workers, praising good work here and suggesting a change there. Often he talked with the architect and artist, Pedro Huisar (pā′drō wēē′cär).

Most of the stones came from the San Antonio River. The metal they had brought with them from Mexico.

Only very skilled workers can make a bell with a beautiful tone. The bells at Mission San Jose were made in Spain, sent across the ocean to Mexico, and then brought overland to San Antonio. This was not an easy task, for a mission bell is very heavy.

The strong walls of the mission were probably built first, in order that the people might have protection from savage Indians. There were five gates, one at each corner, and another on the west, in the front of the church. The west gate is the one that is opened daily now. At each corner is a tower, a lookout for the soldiers. In the walls are loopholes through which the soldiers and trusted Indians could defend those living in the mission from their enemies.

There were living quarters for the soldiers, the Indians, the civil workers, and, nearest the church, for the priests. These, the granary, and the offices were built along the wall, opening upon the plaza (plä′zȧ). The church stands almost in the center of the square.

Under the direction of the patient priests, and

sometimes by their own hands, paths were made. Flowers were planted. Sometimes they were wild flowers transplanted. Other plants grew from seeds they had brought with them. They set out native trees on the mission grounds.

The Spanish priests remembered the many uses of the olive tree in their homeland, so they planted them at the missions here. Always they had a bed of herbs, used both as medicine and for flavoring the food.

Outside the mission walls, great gardens were planted. Here they raised food for this host of people. The exact number varied from time to time, but about four hundred would probably be the average for San Jose. In these gardens they grew squash, beans, pepper, and many of the vegetables we have today.

Always some sugar cane was planted where it would grow at all. The Indians were very fond of its sweet taste, and many times a lazy and stubborn brave could be persuaded to do his day's work by promising him a stalk of sugar cane.

They planted orchards, too—grapes, plums, and peaches. In the fields they grew wheat, corn, and cotton.

These good Spanish priests provided for irrigation. Modern engineers are amazed that they would have known how to install a system so efficient so many years ago.

Poultry was raised—ducks, geese, chickens, and turkeys. These provided meat for the tables of the large mission family.

The mission also owned a ranch. Here they raised horses, cattle, and sheep.

Within the mission walls was a water well. This was for use in case their enemies blocked the water lines from the river.

There was a mill for grinding grains for bread. And there were workshops where the braves made crude tools and the squaws wove coarse cloth for clothing and bedding.

What was a typical day in the mission like?

Early in the morning came the clear, sweet tones of the mission bell. The priests, the Indians, and the more devout workers and soldiers gathered in the chapel. There was morning prayer, and the priests talked to the Indians. They spoke simply, as one would to a small child. Then, the service ended, each went to his task for the day. The old men made arrows; and the old women were assigned the task they all wanted—fishing. The young women spun and sewed, and the young men farmed and tended the stock. The children had chores about the mission to do, but most of their day was spent at lessons.

All day the priests were very busy. There were so many things to teach the Indians: to wear clothing, to bathe and wash their garments, to sleep on beds, to eat at a table. And, always, they were trying to make these child-like people understand about right and wrong.

This was not easy to do. Often the Indians must have tried the patience of these Spanish fathers. They were clumsy at these unaccustomed tasks when they tried. And often they wouldn't try, pretending to be sick.

Then at evening the bells rang again. Again the priests and Indians gathered in the chapel. This time most of the soldiers and families came, too. There was a longer service.

The Indians particularly enjoyed the music. This was something new and delightful, vastly different from their loud, harsh rhythms.

After they left the chapel, there was general merrymaking. The Indians were fascinated with the guitars which some of the soldiers had. In a surprisingly short time, some of the Indians could play them. For a short time each evening, there was music and dancing.

At night the gates were locked. This was done not only to keep enemies out, but also to keep the Indians from running away. It took many days of patient re-telling to make them understand what the priests were trying to teach them. Many of them never did understand; but some did become both civilized and Christianized.

Let us look now at the most beautiful building in the mission, the church.

The architect and artist who spent a life's work on San Jose was Pedro Huisar (pā'drō wēē'cär). He was sent to do this work by the king of Spain. His forefathers had helped to do the delicate carving on the Alhambra (äl häm'-brä), a beautiful palace in his homeland.

To tell of all the beautiful stone carving in San Jose Mission would take a long time. You will want to see it for yourself some day, anyhow. The most famous piece of work is "The Rose Window." Lovely roses, carved in stone, twine about this beautiful window.

A story, called the "Legend of the Rose Window," has been told for many years.

Pedro Huisar, talented and handsome, was sent by the king of Spain as artist for Mission San Jose. His beautiful lover, Rosa, was to follow later and become his bride. With her trunks of bridal garments, she started the long journey. In a storm on the Atlantic, the ship was sunk. The heartbroken Pedro spent five years carving into the limestone all of his love and sorrow. Around the south window of the mission are roses. The window is called "The Rose Window," in remembrance of the lovely young girl, Rosa.

Some think that the mission bell, hanging high in the tower, has an especially sweet tone. There is a lovely legend told about it, too.

One of the young soldiers at the mission had left a sweetheart in Spain. She had wept when he went away and begged him not to go.

But he was gay and adventurous. He said, "Don't be sad, my dear. I shall be home in a year and you shall have the finest wedding in all Spain."

The young man never returned. He was killed by an Indian arrow.

In a village in Spain, a bell was being cast. It was for Mission San Jose in a faraway land over the sea. A crowd gathered, for casting a bell is a special occasion. A beautiful young girl leaned over the railing and peered into the molten mass. She slipped from her finger a ring, the ring given her by her lover, the soldier at San Jose. Her friends understood, and they, too, dropped in gold jewelry.

According to the story, it is the mixture of metals which gives the bell at San Jose its clear, sweet tone.

Christmas is always a joyous and exciting time. For Mexican-Texans, the season is especially long and gay. The plays which they have at Christmas time were brought from Spain by the Franciscan fathers. They were presented to teach the people the story of the Nativity. They were changed somewhat here, so that now they are part Spanish and part Indian. These plays, very much like the ones held in the Spanish Missions, are given by Mexican-Texans each year now.

Let us pretend that we are one of the Indian children at Mission San Jose many, many Christmases ago. This is probably what we would have seen and done.

Beginning nine days before Christmas, the first *posada* (pō sä′dä) is held. *Posada* is the Spanish word meaning "inn."

So on December 16, the dramatization of Joseph and Mary's search for an inn at Bethlehem begins. At the head of the procession a small platform is carried. Upon it are small figures of Joseph and Mary. The people march two by two. They usually carry lighted candles, and always are singing as they go round and round. As they pass a doorway, they stop. Some one sings, "In heaven's name I beg shelter."

From within there is a sharp reply, "There is no room."

This ends the religious part of the celebration. Then there is a supper and a *pinata* (pēn yä'tä).

Everybody, especially the boys and girls, enjoys the *pinatas*.

A *pinata* is a large earthen jar decorated with tinsel and tissue paper. It is made to look like a person, animal, or plant. Inside the jar are fruits, nuts, candies, and small toys. The *pinata* is hung from the ceiling. Some one is blindfolded and given a long pole. He tries to strike the jar. Usually several persons try before the *pinata* is broken. Then there is a wild scramble.

The *posada* is repeated, night after night. The ninth time will be Christmas Eve, and on that night the door is opened and the figures of Joseph and Mary are brought in.

On Christmas Eve begins another series of plays called *Los Pastores*. These Spanish words mean "The Shepherds."

Beforehand a *Nacimiento* (nä′cē mē en′tō), or Manger Scene, will be prepared. All the players for *Los Pastores* are in colorful costumes. They, too, sing their parts. The play is usually given outdoors. One can almost believe the players are "real" while watching them by the light of the twinkling stars.

An angel announces to the shepherds the birth of the Christ Child. They start to find him. On the way they meet *diablos* (dē ăb′lōs) who try to prevent their finding the Infant Jesus. The shepherds march and keep time with decorated staves that tinkle with bells. At last they find the Christ Child, and both the shepherds and guests kneel to worship him.

After this religious service there are refreshments for all.

Los Pastores is given every evening until the sixth of January.

And so the children and the grown-ups in the Spanish missions kept Christmas long, long ago. Mexican-Texans keep it the same way today. Have you ever seen the play, *Los Pastores,* or a *posada?* Have you ever taken part in one?

The Franciscan fathers worked in Texas for more than a hundred years. Then the government called them back to Mexico and divided the land among the converted Indians. With no one to care for them, the missions became dirty and soon needed repairs.

Pedro Huisar was given land near the mission. He married an Indian girl. Some of his descendants live on that same land today.

Finally, in 1931, the Franciscan fathers returned to San Jose. Today, as of old, they conduct regular services in the church of the Mission.

Citizens of San Antonio have built an outdoor theater near San Jose Mission. It is called the Huisache (wē sä′chā) Bowl. Here a colorful Fall Festival and Mission Play are held each year, as well as other meetings.

Mission San Jose is a State Park and a National Historic Site. Every day people from all parts of the United States come to see the

Queen of the Missions

USING THE DICTIONARY

Find the following words in the dictionary:

amazed	festival
efficient	granary
engineer	irrigation

molten
plaza
poultry
pretend
transplanted
unaccustomed

Find these words in the story, "Queen of the Missions."

Ask your teacher to play for you *Ave Maria;* Schubert. It was music similar to this to which the Indians listened in the missions so many years ago.

Most of the Spanish priests who worked in Texas were Franciscan Fathers, or followers of St. Francis of Assisi.

Two books about St. Francis which you will enjoy are:

God's Troubadour; Sophie Jewett; Thomas Y. Crowell Company, New York.

Princess Poverty; Sara Maynard; Longmans, Green and Company, New York.

THE FATHER OF TEXAS

No other state owes so much to one man as does Texas to Stephen Fuller Austin. For this reason he is called The Father of Texas.

When Sam Houston was eight months and one day old, another baby boy was born in Virginia. They named him Stephen Fuller, and the town was Austinville in Wythe County.

Mr. Moses Austin, his father, was a native of Durham, Connecticut and of distinguished English ancestry. His mother was, before her marriage, Miss Maria Brown of Philadelphia. From her Stephen inherited his regular features and violet blue eyes. Both parents were well educated. The family consisted of three children—Stephen Fuller, the eldest, Emily Margaret, and James Brown.

When Stephen was six years old, the family moved to Missouri, where his father bought lead mines.

Missouri was at that time a frontier. At the place where the Austins settled, there were many French Canadians and others from New Spain, or Mexico. Little Stephen often saw the Indians galloping over the prairies, chasing herds of buffaloes, and heard their terrible war whoops. When he was eight years of age, a large band of Osages attacked the settlement, intending to rob Mr. Austin's house and store and kill all the whites found there. But Mr. Austin expected them, so was prepared. He turned a small cannon on the savages, who quickly fled to the woods.

Stephen's father built a comfortable home, quite a mansion for its day. He named it Durham Hall, after his faraway childhood home.

Both Mr. and Mrs. Austin were determined that their children should have a good education, although there were few schools in Missouri. First Stephen, like his sister and younger brother, studied at home, his mother being the teacher. Then Stephen was sent to Springfield, Missouri, to study under Rev. Horace Holley, a minister and a very learned man. When he was only eleven years old, this gifted boy was sent to a boarding academy in Connecticut, his father's old home. His studies were completed at Transylvania University, Kentucky, from which

Before Austin accepted a family, they had to stand a rigid test.

he graduated with honors when he was only seventeen years of age.

His school days over, Stephen returned to Durham Hall and went to work in his father's business. The nearest market for the products of their mine was New Orleans. When Stephen was nineteen his father put him in charge of a boat and started him to the Crescent City. Although he was only a boy, and the crew under him were men many years older, he was able to get their cooperation by winning their friendship and respect.

Everyone who knew Stephen Fuller Austin agreed that here was a most unusual young man. He was slender and broad-browed, with even features. His hair was dark brown; his deep-set, thoughtful eyes were of violet blue. Although of small stature, his well proportioned, erect body seemed to take on some of the bigness of his character. Nobody ever called him a little man.

Because he was kind and gentle in disposition, a hard worker, fair and honest, and equally at home with the most polished gentleman or unschooled frontiersman, Austin won the good will of his neighbors. When he was but twenty years of age he was elected to the Missouri legislature.

They were so well pleased with him that he was returned again and again for six years.

Austin now moved to Arkansas. His good name followed him. The people here soon learned to love and trust him as those at his old home had done, and within a year he was elected judge.

About this time the elder Mr. Austin, by the failure of the Bank of Missouri, lost everything he had. At the age of fifty-five he found himself a poor man, forced to begin life over again. He had heard glowing accounts of Texas, and resolved to investigate them.

When Moses Austin reached San Antonio, he was received coldly by the Spanish governor. Greatly disappointed and more discouraged than he had ever been in his life, he was crossing the public square on his way back to the place where he had left his horses.

A large man bowed in greeting.

"Are you Moses Austin?"

"I am."

"I am Baron de Bastrop (bäs trō'). We met several years ago when I was traveling in the United States. Don't you remember?"

Mr. Austin did remember. They talked of this and that.

Then the Baron said, "You look downcast. What has happened? Can I help you?"

Austin told him of his plans, his disappointment, and that he was on the way home now.

But Baron de Bastrop said no, not until tomorrow.

"Come home with me for the night. Governor Martinez (mär tē'nās) is my friend. Let us go together to see him tomorrow."

The next day the governor saw the matter quite differently. He thought Senor Austin's plan most excellent. Spain would welcome good families from the United States.

Moses Austin started the long, weary ride home on horseback with a glad heart. It was only a few days before Christmas. Before he had traveled far, a cold rain drenched him to the skin. Then a cold norther blew, and his clothes froze upon him. He took pneumonia and died soon after his arrival home. One of his last requests was that Stephen should carry out his plans.

Stephen was in New Orleans. A little reluctantly, he set out for Texas. After all, he hadn't planned to spend his life in a wilderness. But his love for his father made it impossible not to do what he had asked.

The governor received him kindly. He was surprised that Senor Austin was so young! But he might choose his own land. There was plenty.

It was summer. Traveling over land that is now embraced in twenty-three counties, Austin explored the lower valleys of the San Antonio, Guadalupe (gwä dä lo͞o′pā), Colorado, and the Brazos. He saw rolling hills and fertile prairies. He saw huisache (wē sä′chā) and mesquite. He saw great liveoaks, draped in moss. He often rode through fields of wild flowers. He heard the songs of the birds. He drank the water from the clear streams. By day he traveled in bright sunshine and at night he slept under the stars.

Before Stephen F. Austin had selected his first grant of land, he had learned to love the country. In his imagination he could see it inhabited with *good* people—*good* as the land was *good*—with farms and towns and schools and churches. Here, he knew, lay his life work.

Austin chose the rich lands between the Brazos and Colorado rivers, south of the old San Antonio Road, and extending to the coast. Transportation by water was easier and safer from the Indians. This area, with its rivers flowing into the Gulf of Mexico, could be reached by boat.

Now to get the right colonists! Austin was an able writer. He wrote an interesting and accurate description of the country, stated the terms, and had his account published in various newspapers in the southern states. Letters began pouring in. But before Austin accepted a family they must stand a rigid test.

"Have you ever been convicted of a crime?"

"Can you furnish a certificate of character from a responsible citizen in your present home?"

If the would-be Texan colonist could give the right answers to these and other questions, he was welcome to come and bring his family. Otherwise, he could stay where he was, or else slip over the border and live elsewhere than in Austin's colony!

In an old letter, written by Austin in 1823, we read:

"No frontiersman who has no other occupation than that of a hunter will be received—no drunkard, nor gambler, nor profane swearer, no idler, nor any man against whom there is even probable grounds of suspicion that he is a bad man."

The first three hundred colonists were selected. They landed on New Year's Day, 1822, on the banks of the lower Brazos.

The first three hundred families in Austin's colony came to be known as The Old Three Hundred. They are like the Pilgrims. They are the forefathers of Texas. There are many good people living in Texas today who are proud to say that they are descendants of a family of The Old Three Hundred.

Austin later secured other land grants and brought many more families to Texas. As empresario (ām prā sä'ryōs), he had almost complete authority. He was lawmaker, judge, and sheriff all in one. Yet, never did one with so much power rule so kindly and so fairly. The colonists loved him and respected his judgment. As for him, Austin wrote to his brother-in-law in a letter, "I feel almost the same interest for their (colonists') prosperity that I do for my own family—in fact, I look upon them as one great family who are under my care."

Time proved that in most of the colonists Austin had chosen wisely. At San Felipe de Austin no houses were locked, not even the stores. In eighteen months there was only one theft. But occasionally someone did get in who was rowdy or dishonest. In that case, Austin did not hesitate to banish him—and pronto!

Pronto (prōn′tō) is the Spanish word meaning quickly.

In those first years the Indians gave the colonists much trouble. They stole everything they could find, especially horses. Sometimes they attacked and killed anybody unlucky enough to be at their mercy.

Often Austin led the men in Indian fights. Once the Indians stole so many of their horses that the colonists had to borrow other horses to pursue them. Austin and a band of about thirty men followed the Indians and captured them. They demanded that the chief punish the guilty ones. Austin ordered each thief to receive fifty lashes. One-half of the beating was to be given by the chief, and one-half by the Texans.

The lash was lightly laid on by the chief, but the braves pretended to faint from pain. However, as soon as the Texans began to apply the lash, they at once recovered from their fainting fits and began to howl with real pain.

After the whipping, the Texans shaved off half the hair on each Indian's head. The colonists were not bothered by this tribe of Indians again for a long, long time.

Austin made two trips to Mexico City. He was falsely imprisoned on the second trip. His health was permanently injured by the long months in the dungeon.

Austin knew he would be in danger if he went to Mexico. One of his friends spoke of it while he was preparing for the journey and he replied that it was his duty to serve the people of Texas.

Once when he was working so hard, a man said to him, "Why do you work so hard? You will never reap the benefits of your labors."

Austin looked him straight in the eyes, and kindly answered, "I know that. But those who live after me *will* reap the rewards of my work."

When the war started, the soldiers (who were the colonists, mostly) made Austin Commander-in-Chief of the Army. He said he was unfitted for leading the army. He urged that they make Sam Houston Commander-in-Chief in his stead, which they did.

But there was another important task for Austin. There was no money at all to arm and feed the army. Stephen F. Austin and his friends, Dr. Archer and William H. Wharton, went to the United States. In New York, Cincinnati, Louisville, Nashville, Mobile, New Orleans, and other places men and money were raised and hurried to the aid of the struggling Texans at home.

"Austin is doing wonders among us for his country," says a writer of that day. "He is a Franklin in patience and prudence."

And then at San Jacinto the Texans won their freedom. Austin was happy; his people were free.

In September the election for President of the Republic was held. Friends put Austin's name on the ballot, but he had been out of the country almost three years and was unknown to those who had come to Texas during that time. Too, Sam Houston's military glory was fresh in the minds of the people. Sam Houston was overwhelmingly elected.

Sam Houston knew he needed Austin's help in setting up the framework of the new government. He asked Austin to be Secretary of State. His answer was what it had always been when he was called upon to serve Texas, which he once called his "bride."

He worked far beyond his strength in a poorly heated room. On Christmas Eve the doctor said the cold had become pneumonia. In his delirium, he talked of Texas. His last words were:

"The independence of Texas is recognized! Dr. Archer told me so!"

On December 27, 1836, at the age of forty-three years, Stephen Fuller Austin died. He was buried at Peach Point; but in 1920 the body was removed to the state cemetery in Austin, the capital city which bears his name.

Such a man was Stephen F. Austin, the
Father of Texas

GOOD THINKING

Stephen F. Austin was respected for his straight thinking. He had a large vocabulary (vō kăb′ū lā-rў). That is, he knew the meaning of many words.

If you don't know exactly what these words mean, look them up in the dictionary in the back of the book. Make sentences using the following words:

native	academy
distinguished	cooperation
inherited	disposition
frontier	reluctantly
prepared	fertile
occupation	delirium

Why was it a wise choice to make Houston Commander-in-Chief of the Army and to send Austin to the United States to seek aid?

THE MOTHER OF TEXAS

Everybody in Natchez, Mississippi, said that Jane Wilkinson was the prettiest girl in town. She was sixteen, slender and graceful. Her hair was dark and her eyes were brown. She was friendly and kind, with a ready smile for all.

Jane was an orphan girl, but she lacked for neither love nor luxuries. She lived in the Calvert home, the furnishings of which had been shipped from Europe. Already this town in Mississippi was becoming famous for its beautiful homes and gracious hospitality. And the Calvert home was the center of social life in Natchez.

One morning Jane had just dressed for school. She was wearing a new green silk bonnet. She tied the satin ribbons beneath her chin and arranged her dark curls. Satisfied with what the mirror told her, she started toward the front door.

Dr. Long ran to meet them.

Kian (kē′an), a negro slave about three years younger than Jane, came flying from the kitchen.

"Don't go to school, Miss Jane! Don't go now! A man's just come to see the sick soldier that Marse (Master) Calvert has upstairs."

"What difference does that make to me?" answered Jane. "Men come to see him all the time."

"Yes, Miss Jane, but this is the handsomest man in the whole wide world!"

Jane had no time to ponder Kian's words. Already Mr. Calvert and the handsome stranger were coming down the hand-carved stairway.

Mr. Calvert introduced them. The stranger was a young doctor, an army surgeon, who had come to see the sick soldier. One glance told Jane that Kian had been entirely right.

Dr. James Long, just twenty-one, bowed in greeting. Later, in speaking of their meeting, he said that, on this morning so long ago, Jane was the loveliest sight he had ever seen.

A little later Dr. Long and Jane were playing checkers.

"I'll wager you a pair of gloves I can beat you," cried the young man.

Jane won. Kian said the young doctor tried

to lose just so he would have an excuse to come again.

In a few days Dr. Long returned, bringing a beautiful pair of gloves.

Jane laughed softly. Hadn't this young man known she was playing for fun?

"You owe me nothing. Ladies do not play for prizes."

"Then take them as a gift," said James. Jane thought he was looking especially handsome that day, standing there tall and straight in his soldier's uniform.

In less than a year the young couple announced their desire to be married. Jane's relatives objected at first. It was true that Dr. Long was brave and good, already a successful doctor. But both James and Jane were so young!

About a month later, the time had come for her to choose her guardian. Imagine the surprise of everyone when Jane pointed to Dr. Long and said, "He shall be my guardian."

In May the young couple were married.

Four years later a treaty was signed that changed the lives of young Dr. and Mrs. Long.

Spain, because of early Spanish explorations, claimed both Florida and Texas. Settlers from the United States had moved into both, but many more had gone to Florida than to the new land of Texas. According to the treaty, Florida became a part of the United States, which gave up all claims to Texas.

Just as many people now object to some action of the government, so many persons then said this treaty was not right. In Natchez, particularly, the people were angry.

"What our government should have done," said young Dr. Long, "was to have helped Mexico gain its freedom from Spain, and annexed Texas to the United States. Mexico would be glad to give up Texas if only the Mexicans could have their own freedom."

"That's right, Dr. Long," said the other men. "We could organize a company to help them. Will you lead us?"

Now Dr. James Long had a young wife and a pretty little daughter, Ann. He owned a large plantation and had built up a good medical practice in Natchez. If he thought only of his own welfare, there was every reason why he should stay at home.

But he could help so many people by the other choice—at least he hoped he could. Should he try?

He talked with Jane about it. There might be hardships for her, he said.

Jane was proud that the people wanted her husband to be their leader. She was proud that he was unselfish and wished to help his fellow-man. They were young. They could stand a few hardships, she laughingly said.

Soon all was ready. Wealthy merchants had supplied the company well. About seventy-five men left with Dr. Long, and before they reached Nacogdoches (năk′ŏ dō′chĕz) the number had increased to almost three hundred.

There was the same flaw in Long's expedition that there had been in La Salle's—the men. Some of these men had come along hoping for personal gain.

The day Dr. Long and his men left, all Natchez gathered to see them off. Jane stood in the crowd with Ann in her arms and faithful Kian at her side.

"Wave good-by to Father," said Jane. Little Ann waved, Jane threw a kiss, and the men were gone.

When they got to Nacogdoches, some of Long's "soldiers" began to plunder and rob the people. This was the beginning of a long series of disappointments for him.

Dr. Long had left Jane a task to do. Perhaps he did this in order that she might be busy and not so lonely. He had asked her to make a flag for his "army."

As soon as her husband had gone, Mrs. Long began rummaging through boxes and trunks, looking for colored silks. The finished flag was a red and white banner. It had thirteen red and white stripes like those of the United States flag, and the union was a single white star on a field of red.

Jane decided to join her husband. She, four-year-old Ann, and Kian started out. They traveled by boat, carriage, and horseback. For two days they were in a downpour of rain. It was a long, hard trip. At last she reached Nacogdoches.

Dr. Long ran to meet them.

"You're just as pretty as ever!" he said. "And Ann, how you've grown!"

The family was happy to be together again. For three wonderful weeks the Longs were in Nacogdoches.

Then Dr. Long, or General Long, as he was called now, had to go to Galveston. He wanted to establish a fort which would serve as a place of landing for colonists coming by water.

Dr. Long called on Jean Lafitte (lä fēt′), the

pirate. Lafitte was polite, but would take no part in Long's plans. Lafitte was trying to make money—nothing else.

However, the pirate did agree to see that none of his men disturbed the fort which Long proposed to build on Bolivar (bŏl'ĭ vär) Point, just across the bay from the island on the mainland.

When arrangements had been made, Long started back for Nacogdoches. On the way he met a friendly Indian, bearing a letter from Mrs. Long. She told him of a Spanish army sent against them. The townspeople had fled. The "soldiers" had deserted. She was at the home of Mr. Brown. She advised her husband to stay away, lest his own life be in danger.

Stay away! This was no time for a man to stay away, when his family was in danger! He swung into his saddle and rode, hard and fast, toward Nacogdoches.

He arrived a few hours ahead of the enemy. There was just time to rush his wife, Ann, and Kian across the Sabine and to safety.

When General Long left for Bolivar again, Mrs. Long, Ann, and Kian were with him. When they came into the harbor at Galveston, they saw loaded ships at anchor.

A messenger from Lafitte came aboard their

ship. Would General and Mrs. Long dine with him?

"Jane, you know I must look after setting the fort in order. I wish we could accept this invitation. It is not every day that one is invited to dinner by a rich pirate! Besides, he may have decided to help us."

"James, dear, why not let me go alone? I know your plans. I can discuss our work with him if he offers to help."

"So you can, dearest. Accept the invitation. It will be something to tell our grandchildren."

And so it was! Years later Mrs. Long's grandchildren loved to hear her tell of dining with the famous pirate, Jean Lafitte.

When she returned home, her husband was eager to know all that had happened.

"We had an elegant dinner," said Jane. "Lafitte has the courtly manners of a true Frenchman. Only his eyes tell of adventure. James, his eyes remind me of lightning in a gulf storm."

That night Jean Lafitte and his men left those shores forever.

The colony at Bolivar Point grew. Life was very pleasant for a time. Ben Milam joined them, and he and Dr. Long became good friends. Dr. and Mrs. Edgar, Dr. and Mrs. Allen, and others at the fort were interesting companions. They enjoyed the scenery. Fishing was a favorite sport. Ann played with her dog, which she had named Galveston. She picked up shells and ran along the sandy beach. Kian was always close by to warn her if she went too near the water.

Then, in 1821, Mexico won her independence from Spain. Long was delighted. He had gone against the Spanish in at least one battle. He expected Mexico to be very grateful for the help of his colony.

"I must go to Mexico City, Jane. I must have an understanding with the new Mexican government."

The men in authority in Mexico City did not greet him as a friend. No doubt part of the misunderstanding was caused by their not being able to speak the same language. General Long was arrested. Later he was set free, only to be killed for some unexplained reason by a Mexican soldier.

Dr. James Long's stormy life was ended at twenty-seven years. His brave young dream had failed—at least for a while.

In the meantime, what was happening at Bolivar Point?

Days passed. The warm days became cooler. It was autumn. The soldiers became restless. Not even Mrs. Long's brave smile and witty jokes cheered them now.

Then it was winter, one of the coldest the Gulf Coast country has ever known. A few at a time, all the soldiers left. They begged Mrs. Long to go with them.

But she answered, "My husband will return and expect to find me here. I shall stay."

At night Mrs. Long and Kian could see the fires of the Karankawa (kă răng'kä wä) Indians on Galveston Island. At dawn each day Jane herself would fire the cannon to let them know there was artillery at the fort. Having no flag, she raised her red flannel petticoat. There it waved in the Gulf breeze for the Karankawas to see. They believed the fort was heavily guarded, so let them alone.

They had little food, living mainly on fish which Kian caught from the bay.

That winter the bay froze over. In the four hundred years since Cabeza de Vaca made his first record of Texas, it has been recorded that the waters of the bay froze only one other time. A bear walked on the ice from the island to Bolivar Point. Mrs. Long, Ann, and Kian watched him shamble along. Ann laughed when Galveston barked at the bear. The dog made a funny sight, skating on the ice—always at a safe distance from the bear, however.

During that cold winter Ann's little sister was born. Mrs. Long named the baby Mary James, the last name being for the baby's father. She was the first Anglo-American child born in Texas.

Mary James was born December 21, 1821. Although the little group at Bolivar Point did not know it, Austin's Old Three Hundred, that very day, were moving up the Brazos River, looking for a place to land.

In the early spring Mrs. Long learned of the death of her husband. Only then would she leave Bolivar Point. Jane Long was a widow, and only twenty-two years old.

The good people of Austin's colony heard of Mrs. Long's plight. They asked her to join them and helped her move.

Mrs. Long lived in San Felipe, Brazoria, and Richmond. In each of these towns she had a hotel, or boarding house. Kian was always with her mistress, and her good cooking contributed to the great success of Mrs. Long's hotels.

In an old letter we read: "At the head of the

social life in San Felipe is Mrs. Long. She is beautiful, delicate, and graceful. And yet she has the energy and business judgment of a man."

Mrs. Jane Long took a land grant in Austin's colony. On her land stood the old fort in the bend of the Brazos River. The county, Fort Bend, is named for this fort, built as a trading post.

When Austin returned from Mexico after his long imprisonment, Mrs. Long gave a dinner in his honor. All the important men of the colony were invited. Austin made a speech. He told them the time had come for Texas to declare herself a free country. And he also gave them a first-hand account of the lively battle of the Texas Navy, at Velasco, only a few days before.

The baby born at Bolivar Point died, but Ann grew to be as lovely as her mother. She married in Richmond, and some of her descendants live there today.

Kian had four children. One of her granddaughters, also named Kian, attended Mrs. Long with loving care as long as she lived.

Mrs. Long was famed for her gracious hospitality. She had many friends, among them Mr. and Mrs. Mirabeau Lamar (mē′rä bō lä mär′).

Lamar is called the Father of Education in Texas.

Mrs. Long had several offers of marriage from worthy men, but she refused them all. All of her love, she said, belonged to that kind and gay young dreamer, Dr. James Long.

Jane Wilkinson Long lived to be eighty-two years old. Even when she was an old, old lady she was witty and charming. She is buried at Richmond, where she lived so many years. The state has erected a marker in her honor at her old home near Richmond.

Because Mrs. James Long was not only beautiful but also brave and good, she is still loved today.

She is often called the

Mother of Texas.

QUESTIONS FOR YOU

1. Where is Natchez? Find it on the map. For what is Natchez, Mississippi, famous?

2. What does "gracious hospitality" mean?

3. Is friendship between Mexico and Texas, in part, the fulfillment of Dr. Long's dream?

4. This is a good story for telling. Learn to tell the story.

SAM HOUSTON

At Timber Ridge Plantation, seven miles from Lexington, Virginia, lived Major Samuel Houston with his beautiful wife Elizabeth, his large family of children, and the usual number of slaves.

Major Houston had been one of George Washington's most valuable officers in the Revolutionary War. He liked army life better than working on the plantation. At the close of the war he had stayed in the army, so was often away from home. But on the occasional evenings with his family he loved to tell his boys of how his father before him had lived on Timber Ridge Plantation and of how his grandfather had sailed from Belfast, Ireland, and in mid-ocean had foiled the dishonest plotting of a pirate on board.

Major Houston was home March 2, 1793. On that day another son was born.

Young Sam liked to fish with the Indians.

"He is a fine boy, Major Houston. He will be a big man, like you," said the doctor.

So they named him Samuel for his father, but everybody called him Sam Houston.

Sam had five brothers and three sisters. They attended a school their father had built for them and the other children of the neighborhood. Sam always had the best part on the school programs. According to his Black Mammy, he was the "speakingest boy in Virginia." He read everything he could get his hands on, especially books on geography and poetry. But in some of his other lessons he was a poor student. School was held only when a teacher could be found, which was only now and then. When Sam Houston was thirteen years old, he had gone to school but six months in all.

At this time his father died. The plantation had to be sold for debts, and Mrs. Houston took her brood across the mountains to Maryville, Tennessee. Cousin Jim Houston already lived there, and he befriended the family in many ways.

By hard work and good management Mrs. Houston and the older boys made the farm prosper and bought stock in a general store. But Sam didn't like to work on the farm. His mother put him to work in the store. That was not to his liking, either. In fact, it seemed that about all young Sam did like to do was to read Homer's *Iliad* or hunt or fish with the nearby Cherokee Indians. His hard-working brothers thought he should do his share of the work, and they told him so! And Sam didn't like that, either!

One day Sam took a book and his rifle and strolled away from Maryville. He lived with the Indians almost three years. The Cherokee Chief had only daughters. Often he had wished for a son. He adopted young Sam as his own son, and gave him the name Colonneh (cō lŏn′-neh), or the Raven. The eagle, he said, was Sam's medicine-animal, or omen of good luck.

The Cherokee Chief understood about Sam' wanting to rest much better than the older brothers had.

"How old?" he said. "Not quite fifteen? How tall? Nearly six feet? You grow too fast, like sap in a tree."

So Sam spent the days in pleasant leisure, and became wise in the ways of the woods and birds and beasts.

Now and then he would return to visit his family and friends. But always he would go back to the Indians, laden with presents. The gifts he had charged at the local store.

When Sam was seventeen, the chief called his young men about him and gave them some good advice. He told them to try to become more like the white men and to learn from them better ways of living.

Sam thought about the old chief's words.

"What about me?" thought Sam. "If the Indians should become more like the white man, should I, a white man, live like an Indian?"

So Sam went home to take up his work as a member of the family and an American citizen. The first thing, he must pay his debts. The bill for the gifts to the Indians was almost a hundred dollars.

What should he do? Sam announced that he would teach school. Sam Houston teaching school! Many poked fun, and called it Indian University. But teach school Sam did—and well, with the split-log benches filled. Within a few months the debts were paid.

The War of 1812 was on. Sam Houston enlisted. As he was leaving home, his mother slipped a ring on his finger. Inside was engraved the single word, "Honor."

He fought under General Andrew Jackson,

distinguishing himself for bravery in the battle of Horseshoe Bend. At the same time he won a warm and loyal friend for life—Andrew Jackson.

After the war, Sam began to study, or "read" law, as it was called, in Nashville. He astonished everyone by passing his examinations in six months. He heard there was a good opening for a lawyer in Lebanon, thirty miles east of Nashville, so he hung out his shingle there.

Sam was grown-up, a handsome young man, fair and tall, with wavy chestnut hair and merry blue eyes. He had a rich, warm voice and a ready, clever answer. Sam liked good clothes, and all his life he wore them. A friend in Lebanon extended him credit. Sam was quite a dashing figure in costumes of the finest cloth and latest fashion.

"Six feet six," they said of him. Actually Sam Houston was six feet three; but his strong personality made him seem even bigger, so "Six feet six" became a popular legend.

About this time there was trouble with the Indians. Sam Houston, who understood his red brothers so well, was invaluable in getting differences settled. His service won for him many friends. He became congressman from Tennessee, then in 1827, governor of the state. A year later, his good friend Andrew Jackson became President of the United States.

Then at the height of triumph, Sam Houston's colorful life changed abruptly.

Brokenhearted from a shattered romance, Sam Houston turned his back on civilization and went to live in the wigwam of his Cherokee father. He became ill of malaria and almost died. When he was most discouraged, he chanced to see an eagle in the sky. His medicine-animal, his omen of good luck! Perhaps there would be brighter days again.

Houston found his Indian friends in great trouble. Their lands were infringed upon by white men who settled upon them without legal right. The government's Indian agents tricked and cheated them. Dressed in an elaborate Indian costume, The Raven went to Washington on behalf of his red brothers. With the help of the Great White Father, President Andrew Jackson, he was able to secure for them fairer treatment.

That year Sam received a message from Tennessee that sent him hurrying home. His mother smiled lovingly at her son, and pressed the hand that wore her ring with the motto in it. And then she died.

Everyone soon noticed that a change had come over Sam. Perhaps he was thinking of that word "Honor" engraved in the ring he wore. At any rate, he decided to be a white man again and regain the name he had lost.

Andrew Jackson asked his trusted friend to go to Texas on a mission to the Comanche Indians. It turned out that he liked the country well enough to stay and make Texas his new home. An incident of his leaving leads us to believe that Houston was giving such a decision consideration even before his arrival in the land of the Tejas.

As Sam was leaving, a friend in Arkansas rode a little way with him. He wished to give his friend, Houston, a parting gift, but had only a razor to offer. As Sam accepted it, he said, "This razor may some day shave the President of a Republic." And so it did.

On December 2, 1832, Sam Houston crossed the Red River. Looking upward, he saw an eagle against the blue Texas sky.

Houston stopped in Nacogdoches to see his friends, the Wharton brothers. Then he rode on horseback to San Felipe de Austin to meet Stephen F. Austin, the most important figure in Texas.

Never was there a more striking contrast between two men than between Houston and Austin. Austin, small of stature, scholarly, and idealistic; Houston, a husky giant of a man, impulsive, dashing, and colorful. And yet, never were there two men who more sincerely respected the abilities of the other.

Relations between the Texan colonists and the Mexican government grew steadily worse. On March 2, 1836, a convention was called at Washington-on-the-Brazos.

In a blacksmith shop, chilled to the bone by a typical "blue norther," delegates declared Texas free and independent from Mexico. Sam Houston was among them, and signed his bold signature to the Declaration. The Convention elected him Commander-in-Chief of the Army of Texas.

March 2, 1836, was a very busy day. There was no time to mention that this was Sam Houston's forty-third birthday.

As he rode away, he went to one side of the road and put his ear to the ground. This was a trick he had learned from the Indians.

"The cannons have ceased firing," Houston said. "The Alamo has fallen."

And it had.

Houston took command of the army at Gonzales. Never was there another army like this one. There were only a few hundred men, and of that nobody ever took an accurate count. They had no uniforms, but wore whatever they had to wear. Many of them provided their own weapons of war, and a motley assortment it was. To add to this unmilitary-like appearance, women and children, refugees seeking protection, were traveling with the army. Some of them carried their household furnishings with them.

Houston was retreating before the Mexicans until he could organize his "Army." He hoped, too, to get Santa Anna's forces separated. He knew these few men couldn't possibly fight the whole Mexican army. But if he could manage to get Santa Anna separated from his main forces, and take him captive, he would win not only a battle but the war.

That is just exactly what he did do. At San Jacinto all was as he had hoped it would be. Houston knew that at midafternoon the Mexican officers would be enjoying a siesta. Santa Anna was sound asleep in his carpeted tent. Quietly the Texans crept forward, and at the signal of command rushed forward upon the surprised and wholly disorganized army. In only eighteen minutes the Texans won their victory.

And so was born the Republic of Texas on April 21, 1836, on the Battleground of San Jacinto. In September the people went to the polls to choose their first President. This honor went to the hero of San Jacinto, Sam Houston.

At the end of his first term as President, Houston made a trip to the United States. Near Mobile, Alabama, he met beautiful Miss Margaret Lea. She was intelligent, well educated, and an excellent musician.

The next spring he returned to marry her.

Margaret loved her husband dearly. She shared, too, his love for the struggling young Texas. With her encouragement, the comforts of home, with bright flowers outside and music within, Sam Houston was happier than he had ever been before. When his first child was born, this grizzled old warrior and able statesman was as light-hearted as a boy.

Sam Houston was twice President of the Republic, twice governor of Texas, and for fourteen years Congressman from Texas to the United States Senate.

Then came the Civil War. Houston knew

secession would bring only suffering and defeat, so he strongly advised against it. Texas seceded March 2, 1861, the anniversary of Texan independence and Sam Houston's sixty-eighth birthday.

It was a sad birthday. Sam Houston was brokenhearted that his old friends had turned against him because of this difference of what each believed to be right. He was grieved because of the hardships which lay ahead for his beloved Texas.

Before the war was over, General Sam Houston became very ill. Dawn of July 26, 1863, found Margaret watching at his bedside. She had sat there all night.

At sunset General Houston ceased to breathe.

Mrs. Houston took the ring from his finger, and held it so her own sons could see the single word, "Honor."

His mother had said, "Remember, Son."

Sam Houston had remembered—all his life.

MAKING A PLAY

There are many interesting and amusing stories about the life of Sam Houston.

You are old enough now to use the library. Search in your classroom library, or your school library, and perhaps even at the public library for other stories about Houston. When you have made your reports to the class, why not have a committee to write a play?

It would be fun to give the play at an assembly program. If you work hard, you may make your play so good you will want to invite your mothers.

THE TEXAS RANGERS

You have read stories about the Texas Rangers. Surely every seventh grade boy and girl knows something already about them. Wouldn't you like to know more about these brave men?

The organization of the *Rangers* is found only in our state. They are called Texas Rangers. Nobody knows exactly how the idea began. Stephen F. Austin mentioned "rangers" in letters that he wrote in 1821. He used the word in the way we would speak of a policeman on duty. Since Texas was under the rule of the Spanish at that time, some believe that Texas Rangers were started by the Spaniards.

Others say the idea originated among the early colonists. This much is a matter of record.

In 1835 a very important meeting was held at San Felipe de Austin. The meeting was called by Austin himself. He wanted the people to know the true state of affairs. He wanted to know what they thought best to do. And he wanted them to work together in making some plans for their protection.

The Comanches—that wild, fierce tribe of Texas Indians—had always been a constant source of danger to the settlers. Now these cunning Indians saw that the people had their hands full defending themselves from Santa Anna's soldiers, and they began to make more frequent raids.

So the people had to make plans for fighting both the Mexicans and the Indians. The army was to meet Santa Anna's soldiers. And the Texas Rangers were organized to fight the Comanches.

Early in 1836 the Rangers began their work. There were three companies of twenty-five men each. One company was to range east of the Trinity River, one between the Trinity and the Brazos, and one between the Brazos and the Colorado.

Captain R. M. Coleman, Captain G. B. Erath, and Captain W. M. Eastland were the first captains. A county in Texas is named for each of these men, so we honor them even today.

These first three captains began selecting their men.

"There they are, boys! Let's go!"

"Each man," said Captain Coleman, "must have a good horse, a good rifle, and a brace of pistols." In addition to this, each man carried one or more knives for hand-to-hand combat. One of these knives was usually a bowie knife.

That was all. Nothing was said about courage. That was taken for granted.

But some one else has said that the Texas Rangers could ride like Mexicans, trail like Indians, shoot like outlaws, and fight to the finish like a Comanche.

And for all of this, these first Texas Rangers were paid $1.25 per day.

The Rangers were undrilled and had no uniform. However, they all wore high boots and big white hats, so now many people believe that was the official attire.

The Texas Rangers were individuals. They fought that way. And they made a good job of it.

Less than two years after his appointment, Captain Coleman died. The tragic fate of his family is typical of what the settlers endured from the Comanches.

Mrs. Coleman and her six children lived near the town of Bastrop. At that time Bastrop was only a small settlement. Their farm was on the prairie, several miles from the closest neighbor.

It was early spring. The two older boys were cutting stovewood some distance from the house. Mrs. Coleman, fifteen-year-old Albert, the two girls in the family, and little four-year-old Thomas were in the field. The morning was sunny and gay. The group in the field talked and joked as they went about their work.

Suddenly there was a warning shout from Albert. He had seen the flash of a feathered head in the wood. The next instant a hundred Comanches charged across the field, yelling like the wild men they were.

The race for the house began. Albert reached the cabin first. He flung the door open for the others to enter. The girls got safely inside.

Little Thomas ran as fast as he could, but that wasn't fast enough. His mother lagged behind to help her little boy. Mrs. Coleman was killed by a barbed arrow. Thomas was carried away by the Indians and never heard from again.

Albert and his sisters bolted the door. We do not know the exact ages of the little girls, but since they were younger than Albert, they must have been about your age. One of them might have been younger. There were three rifles in the cabin. Albert fired time after time as a Comanche started toward the house. His sisters handed him the loaded guns and occasionally brought him a drink of water. They took turns at watching from the other window.

It was afternoon. The children wondered if their older brothers, who had gone to chop wood early that morning, had learned of their plight. They hoped they had gone for help. As the sun sank lower, time after time they scanned the horizon. If only help would come!

Just at sunset Albert was fatally injured. A little later, a group of neighbors, led by the older brothers, dashed across the field. The Comanches, tiring of their sport, rode away. But the Coleman family was vastly different from the happy group they had been that morning.

The cattlemen, too, lived in constant peril from the Indians. The Comanches lived mostly in the western part of the state. The ranchmen, also, lived in that area. It was only natural, then, that they should have had more trouble with the Indians than the people living in East Texas.

In the scrapbook of the family of Than Cannon, a pioneer ranchman of West Texas, we read the following story:

"It was the summer of '68. There were

twenty of us, driving 2,200 head of cattle to Santa Fe, New Mexico.

"Near the foot of the Guadalupe Mountains, we came upon a man, lying face down with an arrow in his back. We knew at once that the herd a day's drive ahead of us had been attacked by Indians the day before.

"We stopped to bury this unfortunate man. Suddenly, fierce war whoops pierced the air. The Indians charged from two sides. We were outnumbered ten to one, but we fought the Indians for more than an hour. Our cattle stampeded, and we lost most of them. Two of our comrades were killed. We said a few words of prayer, and buried them at the foot of the Guadalupe."

Times like these were typical of the everyday life of pioneer cattlemen.

The Comanche raid on the Coleman family and on Than Cannon and his friends were but two of many. Without the valiant work of the Rangers, only heaven knows what might have happened. We still have a saying in Texas, "as wild as a Comanche." And that is very, very wild!

In 1840 the Comanches made the greatest raid of all. This raid is called the Great Comanche

Raid. The Texas Rangers, assisted by a volunteer army, defeated the Indians at the Battle of Plum Creek. The site of the battle is between the present towns of Lockhart and Luling. Captain Matthew Caldwell distinguished himself in this battle. The county is now named for him.

Captain Jack Hays was another brave Ranger. He had a famous saying, "There they are, boys. Let's go!" A county is named for him.

After the Battle of Plum Creek, the Comanches returned to their old home in the Panhandle. They called their leader Chief Quasho. But the Rangers called him Old Iron Shirt.

Old Iron Shirt wore a cuirass (kwē răs′). Nobody knows how the Indian got it. Perhaps it had been worn by one of Coronado's men. At any rate, now, three hundred years later, a Comanche chief was wearing a Spanish cuirass!

Chief Quasho had magic powers—at least he said he did, and his people believed him. He could turn a bullet in its course, so he said. But Old Iron Shirt made one raid too many, for there was one ranger bullet which neither his magic powers nor his cuirass turned.

Captain Sul Ross is often called the greatest

of all the Texas Rangers. He was in charge of the group that captured Cynthia Ann Parker. He was later elected governor of the state. The Teachers College at Alpine is named for him. As one approaches Alpine the name Sul Ross is seen spelled out in stones on a mountain side.

About the time of the Civil War, a new menace appeared on the southern border. Mexican bandits crossed the Rio Grande for the purpose of cattle thieving on a large scale. Now the Rangers had a double duty to perform.

Then came the troubled years after the War between the States. The southern states were governed by men appointed at Washington. The Texas Rangers were abolished. This pleased the Comanches, Mexican bandits, and outlaws very much. It was a hey-day for all of them. The citizens complained bitterly, however.

Officials at Washington thought there must be some mistake. Everybody, they said, knew Indian raids were a thing of the past. But they sent General William T. Sherman to investigate.

He arrived at Fort Richardson, near the present town of Jacksboro. Those at the fort had arranged a splendid banquet for General Sherman. In the midst of their dinner, the Comanches swooped down and raided the government's wagon train. Seven men were killed and many more wounded. General Sherman was convinced! In 1874 the Texas Rangers were again authorized to protect the people.

Sam Bass was an outlaw who robbed and killed in our state about seventy years ago. He and his gang were captured by the Rangers at Round Rock, Texas.

One of the last strongholds of the warring Indians was in the mountains of San Saba. Few Comanches were ever taken prisoners, for they fought to the death. But at San Saba, Little Bull of the Comanches was captured and sent to the penitentiary at Huntsville. He was the only Comanche to serve such a term.

Captain Bill McDonald made a statement that is often quoted about the Rangers.

There was trouble in Dallas. They asked the governor to send the Texas Rangers.

Captain McDonald stepped from the train. The mayor had expected more than one man.

"Where are your Rangers?" he said.

"Rangers!" said the Captain. "I'm here. You've got only one riot, haven't you?"

Years went by. The Comanches no longer

went on the warpath. But there was still work for the ranger to do. Outlaws and criminals were still here. The worst of these were handled by the Texas Rangers.

In 1935, the legislature created the Department of Public Safety, combining the Rangers and the Highway Patrol into one department. The Ranger force today is composed of about six captains and whatever number of privates needed. The good Texas Ranger today has the courage of the Ranger of the old days. And he is also trained in modern methods of scientific crime detection.

The Highway Patrol is composed of a much larger number of men. Their duties are to save lives and prevent accidents by enforcing the laws of traffic safety.

The Comanche Indians believed that every brave who drank water from the Red River would become cunning and wise. Surely our present day Rangers and Highway Patrol must have drunk from Red River. They must be cunning and wise to know the right thing to do each day.

Suppose you and I drink some water from Red River, too. Let's be cunning and wise and keep all the rules of safety! Shall we?

SAFETY RULES

Match the two parts of these safety rules.
(Do not mark in the book.)

Stop, look, and listen	an electrical outlet.
Never overload	animals alone.
Don't get too near	before you cross the street.
Leave strange	glass at once.
Pick up broken	an open fire.
Put sharp	with gasoline.
Don't clean clothes	on stairways.
Be careful	head, not even in play.
Never throw	tools away.
Never hit anyone on the	rocks.

THE STORY OF THE TEXAS NAVY

It was late summer in 1835. The moving waters of the Gulf of Mexico were silver under the soft rays of a full moon. All the world was beautiful and peaceful as the merchant schooner *San Felipe* moved toward Velasco.

But the hearts of those on board were troubled and heavy. Though a vessel of commerce, the *San Felipe* carried on this voyage two guns upon her deck. What would be the next move of the Mexican government? What was the will of the people of Texas? Nobody knew the answer.

On board the merchant schooner were two passengers who loved devotedly this new land of Texas. One was Mr. Stephen Fuller Austin and the other Don Lorenzo de Zavala.

Austin had gone to Mexico as a representative of the people, asking that the government correct certain injustices. He had been imprisoned on a flimsy pretext for two years. Now, pale and worn, he was returning. His heroic attempt to explain the needs of his people and to secure for them their just rights had failed completely. Santa Anna, cruel and egotistic, would listen to no one.

Lorenzo de Zavala was a Spaniard who had come to make his home in Mexico. He was well educated, capable, and honest. He soon had many friends among the high officials in Mexico City. He was at one time private secretary to Santa Anna.

As the two men worked together, soon they both knew they could never agree. De Zavala was honest. Santa Anna was dishonest. De Zavala was kind. Santa Anna was ruthless. After a time Lorenzo de Zavala resigned his position with the government and cast his lot with the newer frontier, Texas.

Austin and De Zavala stood together on the deck. The Spaniard spoke.

"Mr. Austin, the salt air and good food are bringing some color to your face. You looked like a pirate's ghost when you came aboard!"

Both men laughed. When Austin spoke, his voice was low and tense.

“Come and get ’em!”

"I fear that my health is permanently damaged. The only good resulting from my long, dreary imprisonment is that now I am sure of the right course for our people. I know now of Santa Anna's high-handed tactics, even with his own people—his own friends. Texas must now declare her independence from Mexico. I shall so advise the people upon my return."

"And you shall be entirely right, Mr. Austin. Remember that I'm casting my lot with the colonists. I shall be honored to have you call on me, if I can be of assistance."

"Thank you, Señor De Zavala. Your help will be valuable, and will be needed. Goodnight."

"Buenas noches, Mr. Austin."

It was four o'clock in the afternoon of September 1, when the *San Felipe* sailed to the entrance of the port at Velasco. The Mexican sloop-of-war, the *Correo,* lay off the port—waiting.

The *Correo* was commanded by an English sea adventurer in the pay of Santa Anna's government. His name was Thomas M. Thompson, and he was generally known as Mexico Thompson.

The watch on the ship commanded by Thompson sighted the *San Felipe.*

"Cut her out!" barked Thompson.

A merchant vessel was hardly a match for a sloop-of-war. The *San Felipe,* clapping on all sail, made a run for the safety of home port. The race was on.

From the shore Thomas F. McKinney, one of the schooner's owners, watched. He knew something must be done.

"We've got to go out and help her, boys!" he shouted. "Who'll volunteer to go with me?"

A crew was quickly assembled. They all rushed aboard another small steamer in the harbor and went to the aid of the *San Felipe.* While some of the reinforced crew stood ready at the rail with small arms, the Texan merchantman was anchored. But McKinney had his "blood up."

"If it's a fight they want," said the merchant, "they shall have it. But first, Mr. Austin, we're going to put you ashore. You've had enough of Mexican prisons for a while, I suspect. And you'd better go, too, Zavala. I imagine Santa Anna would like to have you with him again."

Stephen F. Austin protested, and so did Zavala, but at last both men were convinced that they could best serve the people by going ashore.

About ten that evening, McKinney knew from the movements of the enemy ship that a fight was coming. The men of the *San Felipe* looked to their weapons and stood ready.

"Ahoy, the *San Felipe!*" came the cry from Mexico Thompson. "Stand by, and send your papers aboard!"

McKinney, cupping his hands to his mouth, shouted back:

"You want our papers? Well, come and get 'em!"

And the fight was on. Just at dawn, realizing that he was beaten, the *Correo's* commander gave the order to sail for the high seas.

"Now let's give her a chase, boys!" yelled McKinney.

But could they overtake the *Correo?*

Just then McKinney sighted a little steamer coming out. On it was almost every able-bodied man in Velasco. They had more ammunition, too. The steamer, being faster than a sailing vessel, towed the *San Felipe* within range of the *Correo.*

Less than an hour later the flag came fluttering down on the *Correo Mexicano.* A wild cheer broke from the deck of the *San Felipe.*

Texas had won her first victory on the high seas. It was a merchantman against a man-o'-war; even more, a merchant schooner without a flag or a government to back its actions.

Even before the colonists were officially at war with Mexico, they began to think about a navy to protect the coast line. The enemy could bring soldiers and supplies more easily by sea than by land. The government had no money to buy ships, so the Provisional Governor Henry Smith gave permission to anyone who owned a ship to prey on enemy commerce. These ships were commonly called the "Wasps of the Sea." Certainly they were small. And they proved themselves good fighters. Like wasps, their attack was powerful.

Then came March 2, 1836, and the Declaration of Independence at Washington-on-the-Brazos. Lorenzo de Zavala was there and was elected Vice-President. Stephen F. Austin, Dr. Branch T. Archer, and William H. Wharton had already been chosen as the most eloquent and persuasive speakers to go to the United States and ask for help. But Austin had advised the delegates before leaving.

At the same time that Sam Houston was made

commander-in-chief of the army, a resolution was passed creating a Texas navy. Four small vessels were purchased—the *Liberty,* the *Independence,* the *Invincible,* and the *Brutus.* As the new government had no money, these ships were bought on credit and operated largely on money from private sources.

The *Invincible* was the fastest and strongest of the four. She carried eight guns. The *Independence* and the *Brutus* each carried eight smaller guns, and the *Liberty* carried four.

With this strength—twenty-eight guns against the combined sea power of Mexico—the first official Texas Navy set out to raise its own particular peal of thunder on the Gulf.

How well that small navy succeeded! And with what spirit! Let us consider together some of its encounters.

Far down the east coast of Mexico, lay a four-gun schooner-of-war, the *Liberty,* her single star flag fluttering in the breeze. It was March 3, one day after the convention had declared Texas free.

"Schooner on the weather quarter!" sang the lookout.

The captain of the Texan ship waited.

"Flies the Mexican flag, sir. I'd say, by her

looks, she's the *Pelicano,"* continued the lookout.

The *Pelicano* she was.

The *Liberty* opened fire, and kept it up fast and furiously. She struck some telling blows. So, hardly without a fight, the *Pelicano* surrendered.

An inventory disclosed that the captured ship was carrying five hundred and fifty barrels of flour and a quantity of potatoes and apples. These provisions had been intended for Santa Anna's soldiers but now they would be eaten by hungry Texans instead.

But not until they reached Matagorda Bay was the prize of the cargo known. While the flour was being unloaded, one of the barrels was dropped. As the staves fell apart, something else rolled out—a smaller keg which had been hidden in the flour.

It didn't take the Texans long to discover what the smaller keg contained—gunpowder! They hastily examined other barrels, and found that they, too, contained kegs of gunpowder.

There was general rejoicing. General Sam Houston was so elated he issued a proclamation to tell the people of the good fortune and to express appreciation to Captain Brown and the men of the *Liberty.*

Then it was April, and the Battle of San

Jacinto was fought and won. Texas was free, and the Texan Navy had a large part in winning the victory. They had brought supplies, munitions, and volunteers from the United States. At the same time, they had prevented Santa Anna from receiving food or reinforcements by sea.

Later the *Invincible* and the *Brutus* were wrecked. The *Liberty* was sent to New Orleans and sold there to pay expenses. The *Independence* was captured by two Mexican ships.

This was the first and only time in the history of the Texas Navy that the flag was lowered in defeat. An interesting story is told of Lieutenant Taylor, who was in command of the ship.

"I am your prisoner," he said, "but my sword you shall never receive."

Then Lieutenant Taylor unsheathed his sword, walked to the rail, and threw it overboard.

When the captured crew of the *Independence* reached Mexico, whom do you think they met? The Britisher, Mexico Thompson! He was very kind to the Texans. In fact, so great was his admiration and friendship for these sailors that a few years later he came to Galveston and joined the Texas Navy.

So, on April 17, 1837, the capture of the *Independence* ended the First Texas Navy.

However, the people of the Lone Star Republic did not forget their navy. Transportation by water was the common custom of commerce. During the administration of Mirabeau B. Lamar, second president of the Republic, the New Texas Navy was launched. The New .Navy was larger, consisting of six large ships and several smaller vessels.

Stephen F. Austin and Lorenzo de Zavala had died during the early days of the Republic, so the two largest ships were named in their honor. The *Zavala* was an eight-gun steamship. The *Austin* was the largest of the fleet and was the flagship.

Some of the other ships of this New Texas Navy were the *Archer,* the *Wharton,* the *San Bernard,* the *San Antonio,* and the *San Jacinto.*

The history of the second Texas Navy is closely related to the story of its brilliant young commander, Commodore Edwin Ward Moore. He is often called "the Nelson of Texas."

Edwin Ward Moore was a native of Virginia. He entered Annapolis at the age of fourteen. After graduation he was sent on a cruise in the Gulf. He anchored at Texan ports, and Moore said later that it was on this tour that he caught the Texas spirit. This was in 1835. When governing officials of the Republic needed a commander of the navy four years later, they remembered this capable and friendly young man, Edwin W. Moore.

The blue-eyed, brown-haired, stocky young sailor resigned his commission in the United States Navy and took command of the Texas fleet.

The new vessels began arriving in Galveston. Commodore Moore and his lieutenants went recruiting, to New Orleans and other cities where sailors seek rest from the sea. Soon the second Texas Navy was ready to raise a new peal of thunder on the Gulf.

Trouble was brewing in the south. Yucatan, a state in Mexico, was revolting against Santa Anna. They offered to pay the Republic $8,000 per month for help from the Navy. This plan pleased both President Lamar and Commodore Moore, so the flagship *Austin* put to sea, and the *San Antonio* and the *San Bernard* followed in her wake.

Our Navy bravely defended the ports of Yucatan. An old letter from one of the officers gives an interesting sidelight. A party was given on one of the English ships. The commander of the *San Bernard* was invited, but could not attend because his uniform was so shabby. The new nation of Texas had very little money to support the navy. But just as the soldiers at San Jacinto had fought without uniforms, so the sailors in the navy were good sailors without new uniforms with shining brass buttons.

Then Lamar's term of office was ended, and Sam Houston again became president. Houston was an army man. The navy, he said, was unnecessary and too expensive. When he could not gain the support of the people on this matter, he caused Congress to pass a secret law which said that the ships were to be sold.

The President ordered the Commodore to bring the ships home to Galveston. The flagship *Austin* lay at anchor at New Orleans. Houston sent order after order. Moore chose to disobey.

There were several reasons why Commodore Moore did not obey. He thought Houston wanted to sell the navy. The Commodore had used much of his own money to keep the ships afloat. Both his personal fortune and his love and loyalty were in the Texas Navy. He was not willing to see it abolished until he was sure this was the will of the people.

Sam Houston was very angry, and his wrath was no light thing. He declared the Commodore and his men to be pirates, and ordered them seized by other nations!

Excitement ran high. Everybody was talking about the matter. Some sided with Houston. Others thought the Commodore had done exactly right. The citizens of Galveston, sharing the sailors' love of the sea, thought the whole matter an outrage. The ladies of the town prepared handsome badges to be presented to the officers of the *Austin* and the *Wharton* when they should come home from the sea.

With a heavy heart the fleet sailed into the Galveston harbor.

From the shore came a salute of twenty-one guns. The Commodore hadn't been sure that courtesy would be extended!

The flagship *Austin* answered with a salute of twenty-one guns.

Then a note from the mayor was sent aboard. What time might Commodore Moore and his men be expected ashore? A jubilee had been planned in their honor.

The "pirates" were coming home as heroes!

This was July 14, 1843.

The ships were never sold. So many people

had opposed selling them that Congress changed its mind. When Texas was annexed, the remaining four ships of the Texas Navy became a part of the United States fleet.

As for Commodore Edwin W. Moore, his name lives on in the state he served so gallantly. Moore County, in the Panhandle of Texas, is named in his honor.

MORE ABOUT SHIPS

The United States Navy is made up of modern ships of various kinds. Our navy is strong and well equipped for protecting our long coast line.

This is how navy ships are named:

Battleships are named for states.

Cruisers are named for cities.

Aircraft Carriers are named for battles or historic naval vessels. (There have been exceptions, as *Franklin D. Roosevelt.*)

Submarines are named for sea animals.

Find out the name of one ship in each of these four groups.

Try to find a picture of one ship in each group.

STORY OF SAN JACINTO

On March 2 Sam Houston was elected Commander-in-Chief of the Army. He went directly to Gonzales, arriving on March 11. Here he found the people in a panic. News of the tragedy at the Alamo had just reached them.

Houston gathered about him a little army of less than four hundred men. Many of them had no guns. There was little food and less ammunition. Houston knew he could not hope for a victory if he met Santa Anna now.

So he began a long retreat, drilling his men along the way. Families were afraid to be left at home unprotected, so they traveled with the army. This is called the Runaway Scrape.

Never before or since was there such an army. The men had no uniforms. They wore whatever clothes they had to wear. Many of the soldiers provided their own arms. Guns and swords were of just about every kind used at that date.

Will You Come to the Bower?*

*"Will you Come to the Bower?" was the song sung by Sam Houston's army at San Jacinto, and the strains of this old air were mingled with the shouts of "Remember the Alamo! Remember Goliad!"

Most of the men had come to Texas from the United States. They had come from as far away as Maine, practically every state in the Union being represented in their ranks. Others had even crossed the ocean to make their home here.

Nine European countries were the homeland of soldiers in Sam Houston's army.

And whoever heard before of an army traveling with women and children and the sick and the aged?

To add to all this discomfort and hardship, the spring rains that come in Texas in late March and April came pelting down.

The commander-in-chief shared all these hardships with his men. He shared the same scanty food. His saddle was his pillow. One blanket served as both mattress and cover. His uniform was a worn leather jacket.

Stephen F. Austin, Dr. Branch T. Archer, and William H. Wharton had gone to the United States to ask for help soon after New Year. Their work was beginning to bear fruit. New recruits were arriving. Boxes of food and ammunition were coming in.

When Houston and his men crossed the Brazos, they found two small cannons on the opposite bank. These cannons were the gift of the people of Cincinnati. The Texan soldiers nicknamed them "The Twin Sisters," and that is what we call them today.

Santa Anna, proud and overly confident, thought he had defeated the revolting Texans.

His egotism made him careless. His forces were scattered. When he crossed the Brazos, he sent some of his soldiers back to Mexico.

At San Felipe he learned that the government had been moved to Harrisburg. Santa Anna thought it would be an easy matter to capture the Texas officials there, and so end the war. He thought with special pleasure of taking revenge on Lorenzo de Zavala, Vice-President of Texas.

Lorenzo de Zavala was a scholarly Spaniard who had lived in Mexico City. He had once been Santa Anna's friend; but when Santa Anna made himself a dictator, Zavala would have no part with him. This fair and honest gentleman came to Texas to make his home.

Santa Anna's army marched on to Harrisburg, and burned the town. But the officials escaped with their important records. The Mexican army marched on to a point near San Jacinto Bay and pitched camp.

In the meantime Houston's scouts had kept him informed of Santa Anna's movements. Everything was just the way he had hoped it would be now. Santa Anna was separated from the larger part of his army. As for the Texas army, it now numbered nine hundred and sixty men. Each man was armed. And the five weeks of drilling had brought some organization to these raw recruits.

Houston followed his enemy. When the Texans passed through Harrisburg, smoke still curled from the burned homes.

Deaf Smith, the very best of all the good Texas scouts, dashed into camp with important news. He had captured a Mexican courier and learned from papers in his wallet that Santa Anna's army was less than ten miles away.

Houston gave the command to march again. The men ached with weariness. The prairies were boggy. It had been backbreaking work to get the wagons and cannons through the mire.

But the men marched with glad hearts. They were fighting to make their country free. They wanted to have this battle over and done with, so they could go home to their families.

The Texas soldiers crossed Buffalo Bayou at night, moving as quietly as they could. Just at sunrise on April 20th, the army took its position. They were on a stretch of rising ground, on the bank of Buffalo Bayou, in a beautiful grove of live oaks. Less than three-fourths of a mile away was their enemy.

Just then several fat head of cattle were seen grazing nearby. In a very short time the whole

Texas army was enjoying juicy beefsteaks for breakfast.

Then Houston spoke to his men.

"You've done good work, boys. You deserve a rest. Take it now."

All that day and night the exhausted men rested. Sleep and beefsteak renewed their energy. They awoke feeling fine next morning.

The morning of April 21st dawned clear and fair.

General Houston rose from his bed on the bare ground.

"The sun of victory has risen again!" he said.

The soldiers said to each other, "Look! The sun of victory shines on us today."

Eyes were bright. Voices were quick and eager. All over the camp there was a strange feeling. It was as though they were saying to each other without words, "This is the day! This is the day we've waited and hoped for!"

At midmorning some men were seen marching in the distance.

"Perhaps they are new recruits joining us!" thought the Texans.

But they were five hundred Mexican soldiers under General Cos, joining Santa Anna's army.

"I'll put a stop to that," thought Sam Houston.

And he commanded that Deaf Smith be brought to him.

At first the old scout didn't understand. A group of the younger soldiers nearby were singing "Will You Come to the Bower?"

Deaf Smith turned his good ear and Sam Houston spoke louder. This time the scout understood.

Sam Houston had said, "Cut down the bridge over Vince's Bayou."

Away rode Deaf Smith. The bridge was as good as down already, and Sam Houston knew it.

It was noon, and still no order to advance. Some of the soldiers were impatient.

"What is Houston waiting for?" they asked.

Sam Houston knew what he was waiting for. He had learned the daily routine in the Mexican army. He knew that in midafternoon Santa Anna and his officers would take a siesta (sĭ-ĕs'tȧ). Had Lorenzo de Zavala told him this? Perhaps. He had given sound advice on other matters. Or had Houston been clever enough to observe this custom? We do not know the answer to these questions.

It was a warm afternoon in spring. The soldiers under General Cos had marched most of the night before. Nearly all of them were asleep now. Santa Anna, in his carpeted tent, was sound asleep. So were nearly all of the Mexican officers. There was no one to command the soldiers to stay busy. Some of them thought they might just as well get a little rest, too. Of the others, some were eating, some were polishing the officers' boots and guns, and some were riding the horses bareback to and from the water.

About 3:30 in the afternoon Houston gave the command to form in the line of battle. Mounting his horse, he rode to the front of the Texas army to lead the attack.

The Texans advanced quietly until they were near the Mexican camp. Then they struck up the tune, "Will You Come to the Bower?" Someone—we don't know who—started the cry "Remember the Alamo! Remember Goliad!"

Then the Texan soldiers advanced with a mighty fury. They went over the breastworks and right into the camp of their enemy. They fought in hand to hand combat.

There was wild confusion in the Mexican camp. One officer gave one command. Another shouted to the men to do something else.

Santa Anna, roused from his slumber, tried to give command, but gave up and fled for his life. The others did the same.

But where were they to go? Vince's Bridge had been destroyed. Behind them was the fury of the Texans and before them the waters of the bayou. Many of them ran headlong toward the water, then plunged into the marshes, shouting, "Me no Alamo! Me no Goliad!"

The battle was won by the Texans in eighteen minutes. This is the shortest decisive battle in the history of the world.

Lorenzo de Zavala's home was just across the bayou. It was turned into an emergency hospital, and the wounded Texan soldiers were taken there.

Six hundred thirty Mexican soldiers were killed and seven hundred thirty were taken prisoners. And yet, on the night of April 21, Sam Houston and his men were disappointed. Santa Anna was not among the prisoners of war.

The next morning Sam Houston chose the men to ride over the battlefield in search of any enemy soldiers that might have escaped. Every man was hoping to capture Santa Anna.

Three men riding together found a Mexican soldier hiding in the tall grass. He was dressed as a private. His trousers were of blue cotton. A coarse blue jacket covered his shoulders. On his feet he wore red worsted house slippers.

The Texans commanded their prisoner to get up and walk before them to camp. As he rose, the blue jacket was parted. They noticed that underneath these old clothes he was wearing a shirt of the finest linen, fastened with jeweled studs.

Could this be *The Prisoner?* Well, they would soon find out.

When the prisoner had walked a short distance, he stopped. He said he could not walk any farther, and begged to ride. Houseshoes were not very well fitted for walking over the rough ground. One of the men said, "Get up behind me."

As they rode into camp, the Mexicans cried, "El Presidente! El Presidente!" It was then that the men knew they had captured Santa Anna.

Houston was lying on a pallet under a great live oak tree. The pain from his wounded ankle had kept him awake most of the night, and now he had fallen into a light sleep. He was awakened by the noise. Santa Anna was brought before him.

The proud "Napoleon of the West" humbled himself before plain Mr. Houston. The war was ended.

A few days later Sam Houston called his men around him.

"Boys, you have won a great victory in the face of many difficulties. Many years from now people will tell their children of what you did here at San Jacinto. Now your work as a soldier is finished. We have here some corn left from our supplies. We shall distribute it as seed corn. It is time to get our crops planted. Go home now, and plow and plant your fields. Let's call this San Jacinto corn, and may its yield be bountiful."

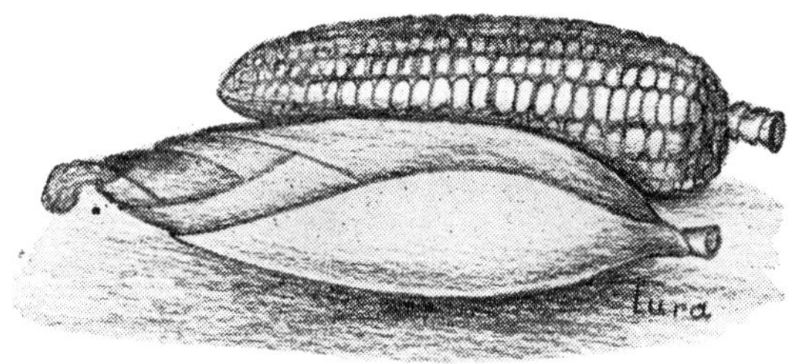

The only flag carried at San Jacinto had come to Texas from Kentucky and was carried by James Austin Sylvester. The flag now hangs, back of the Speaker's stand, in the House of Representatives in Austin.

The San Jacinto Battlefield is a state park. It is not far from Houston, on the highway to Galveston. On the grounds is a beautiful monument that rises 567 feet. It is built of reinforced concrete faced with Texas golden buff limestone. On the ground floor is the San Jacinto Museum of History. On the interior walls are the names of all the brave men who fought in the battle that won freedom for Texas.

HISTORICAL EXHIBIT

Some of you have old and interesting articles in your homes. Would you like to bring them to school and arrange a Historical Exhibit?

You must prepare a place for keeping them safely before you announce the day that articles are to be brought. Number and label each piece carefully so that nothing will be lost.

THE BEST KNOWN LITTLE PIONEER GIRL

It was spring. Nine covered wagons rumbled along, bringing as many families to find a new home in Texas. The children jumped from the back of the slow-moving wagons, played and ran along the beaten trail, which was their road, until they were tired, then climbed back again.

Inside each wagon were the family's most treasured possessions. A few pieces of furniture, a spinning wheel and loom for making cloth to clothe the family, bedding and a pair of cotton cards for making more, iron pots for cooking on a fireplace, a coffee mill, a flint rock to use as we now use matches, a few well-loved family keepsakes, and a family Bible. Father and Mother rode on the seat of the wagon, while the children found any comfortable spot among the household belongings. In almost every wagon

The Indian Chief rode away with the children.

there was some pet, too; usually a cat or a dog. The big hunting dogs trotted along underneath the master's wagon, but occasionally a little boy coaxed his parents into granting permission for Old Blue to ride with the children.

In the first, or lead, wagon rode Mr. Silas Parker. It was he and his father who had persuaded their relatives and friends back in Illinois, to come with them to make a new home in Texas. Grandpa and Granny Parker were traveling with them now.

Already it was midafternoon. The men kept a sharp lookout for a suitable place for camping. You see, pioneers couldn't camp just any place but must find a camp site where there was wood and water. They were driving through big oak trees, so Mr. Parker and his companions knew there was no lack of wood.

"Look!" called Mr. Parker to the man in the wagon behind him. "See how tall this sage grass grows. This is good land."

The wagon wheels ground on. They crossed a stream which we know now as Navasota River. Just as the sun was glowing red they saw, a little to one side, trees of darker green and lacy willows which told them that water was near.

In the back of Mr. Parker's wagon rode his two older children, John and Cynthia Ann.

"Please, Papa," said Cynthia Ann. "Let me run ahead. I'm thirsty for a cool drink."

Her father's permission granted, Cynthia Ann jumped from the wagon. Already her yellow hair stood out in the spring breeze as she ran toward the dark green thicket.

"Be careful, Cynthia," called her mother. "Watch for snakes!"

So Cynthia Ann picked up a stick and beat the grass with a rhythmic motion, going at a slower pace. Other children were coming behind her now. After them came the men, glad to stretch their legs a bit after a long day's travel. Only the mothers with their babies were left in the wagons.

And then they found the water—not a creek, but a spring—a spring of abundant sparkling water. A spring to the pioneers was a great treasure. The water was cool; and on warm days without ice, that was no small thing. The water of this spring was what is called soft water, or free from minerals and therefore good for washing clothes. And best of all, in the days before purification of water, spring water was pure, so could be drunk without fear of sickness.

Cynthia Ann was first to reach the spring. She dipped into its clear, cool depths and drank from her cupped hands.

"It's wonderful!" she called to the others. "Come try it."

And so they all camped there that night.

Next morning they rose early. A camp fire was kindled and each family brought whatever they chose to have for breakfast and cooked it there. It was fun, talking and eating together. Cynthia Ann shared one of her mother's deli cious biscuits with her older cousin, Rachel Plummer and she gave Cynthia some of their cane syrup. The families had been traveling a long time so provisions were getting low.

Red birds flew about in the big trees, singing their cheery songs. While these relatives and friends were eating, a red bird's call came quite near. They looked up at the singer, and were amazed to see a slender grey bird. As they watched, it gave the call of the field lark and burst into a warble resembling a canary.

"What kind of bird can that be?" said Mrs. Parker.

"I've never seen one like it," answered her husband. "That bird can mock anything."

You and I know that these pioneers saw the Texas mocking bird.

It was so pleasant that all the group lingered a little longer than usual after breakfast. As the men drank another cup of coffee, sitting on a log, or a wagon tongue, or just squatting as the cowboys do, Mr. Parker talked things over with them.

"Men, when we left Illinois we said we would find a home with good land and plenty of wood and water. It seems to me that we've found it. What do you say?"

Unanimously the men agreed. They walked over to the cluster of women clearing up after breakfast. Their wives, too, thought this would make a good home.

"Let's tell the children," said Mrs. Plummer.

Reluctantly the children left their play. For many mornings now their play had been cut short by the word that it was time to pack the wagons.

Cynthia ran to her father.

"Please, Papa, can't you wait just a little longer? We've found a big grapevine and we're having lots of fun swinging. You should just see how much farther I can swing than John."

"I swung as far as you did one time," said John. "Silas Bates said I did."

John thought that it just wasn't fair to be younger than your sister, especially when the sister could run or climb like Cynthia.

Mr. Parker smiled. "How would you like to play on your grapevine all day?"

The children were silent and looked at him with surprise and unbelief.

Mr. Parker continued. "How would you like this place for your new home?"

Now the children understood. Their happy shrieks answered for them. Their fathers and mothers smiled. They, too, were glad the new home had been found.

"Children! Children!" said Mrs. Parker. "Not so loud! And stop turning hand springs, Cynthia! Already you're as wild as these Comanches I've heard about—all of you."

But Mr. Parker said, "We'll let the children have a holiday today. In fact, we'll all rest up a bit. Goodness knows, Mother, that you and the other ladies have had it hard enough on the trip. A little sitting in this spring sunshine will do all of you good. We must make the most of today, for tomorrow we start work in earnest and there will be a job for everybody. Now run along, young ones!"

Mr. Parker was right. There was work for even the youngest child to do.

First they cut down trees and trimmed them to make big logs, each fifteen feet long. These were placed side by side to make the walls of the fort about two hundred sixteen feet long, about two hundred feet wide, the walls standing fifteen feet high. In one corner was a huge gate with a hand hewn lock of heavy cross timber. A peep hole with a covered flap made it possible for the person inside to see who stood outside before he unlocked the gate.

At the same corner there was a watch tower, standing eight feet above the fort walls, and here the supply of ammunition and guns was stored. Holes were cut in the walls about four feet apart, all around the tower; and from these the men could sight their guns and fire. A ladder made from smaller logs was nailed to the inside wall, and the pioneer fathers could go up and down it just about as quickly as your father goes up and down stairs.

Then the cabins were built, one for each family. In most of them there was only one large room. They cooked at the fireplace. The few articles brought for housekeeping were set in order. As many extra beds as needed were made from split rails, cut from the many trees all about them. When over this crude frame a comfortable mattress and feather bed were laid, it wasn't so bad. The men made a table to eat their simple meals upon, and benches were made for each of the long sides. In hand-made chairs, the seats covered with cowhide, sat the father at the head of the table, and the mother at the other end, nearer the fireplace, from which she served the meal. The children sat on the benches along the sides of the table.

The houses were set in rows along the sides and end of the fort. At the other end was a large vegetable garden. In the center were flowers and a space for the children to play.

In the early days of the settlement they had some trouble with the Comanches, the wildest and most warlike tribe of Indians in the state. But even the fierce Comanches feared the gunpowder of the white man, so for many months life had moved along at Fort Parker (the people named their fort in honor of their leader) without sign of the red man.

It was spring again. So many days of useless watching and guarding had made the settlers careless. There was no room for the fields within the fort. Their usual plan was for part of the men to stay behind and guard the fort, while other men, armed and alert, went out to work in the fields. The gates of the fort were kept locked, too, being opened only to let the people of the settlement in or out, and then promptly closed and locked again.

As you have already been told, it was spring. If you now live on a farm, or if you have ever even visited a farm in the springtime, you know this time of year is a very busy time for the farmer. Someone, we don't know who, suggested that all the men go work in the fields. After all, they all could have worked yesterday and the day before, and the day before that without any bad results. Hadn't it been months since they'd seen hide or hair of a Comanche? Maybe they had gone far away. And just think how much work there was to do in the fields!

So on May 19, 1836, all the men of Fort Parker went to work in the fields. Some say that a big boy was watching in the tower. Others say that it was an old, old man. Perhaps the women were washing at the spring or working in the big vegetable garden outside the fort walls. At any rate, the gates of the fort were open. As the women and children of the settlement went about their daily tasks completely unaware of the approaching danger, the Comanche warriors crept stealthily forward in the thick woods until they were only three hundred yards from the fort. Then with bloodcurdling yells they dashed into the fort. With savage fury they massacred old and young alike. Someone, we don't know who, ran to the fields to tell the men. Quickly they came to defend their families; but many of them, too, were killed.

Nine-year-old Cynthia Ann and her brother John clung together, horrified. The Comanche Chief walked toward them. We can only imagine the fear of the children. Surely they must have expected the same fate as the others. But, instead, the chief lifted the two children to the back of his own horse and rode quickly away, the other Indians following after their leader.

The few survivors, some of whom were badly wounded, sadly buried their loved ones and friends. Then they set out through the woods to Fort Houston, in what is now Anderson County. This was the nearest white colony, and it was about seventy miles away. It was a trip of many hardships. At last they arrived, ragged and half-starved, their feet torn and bleeding.

Fort Parker was never rebuilt. A few years later a new fort, Fort Springfield, was built about one and one-half miles away. Some of the survivors, among them Silas Bates, returned. Others settled in other parts of Texas, as did John Parker, younger brother of the founder of

Fort Parker. He made a new home in what we know as Parker County. This county is named for Cynthia Ann.

For many years John Parker and others searched for Cynthia Ann and her brother. But when no clue was found they were given up as dead.

Many years passed. Again the Comanches were giving trouble. The tribe had moved westward, and near Pease River in the southern part of the Panhandle, were stealing the ranchers' cattle.

The Texas Rangers were called out to stop the raids of these marauding Indians.

Captain Sullivan Ross, only twenty years old and affectionately called Sul Ross by his men, was sent with a band of Rangers to defend the ranchers. One day one of his men brought in a strange report. He had seen an Indian woman riding beside the chief, her long blond hair flowing behind her. Sul Ross did a quick calculation. This was 1860. Yes, Cynthia Ann Parker would be a grown woman now.

"Men," said Captain Ross, "see that no one fires in the direction of this woman tomorrow. We must take her captive alive and unharmed."

The next day the strange Indian woman with

blue eyes and blond hair was taken captive. Her husband, Chief Nacoma, was killed.

At first the woman could not understand the white man's language. Her uncle, John Parker, came. As he said her name over and over again, she smiled. Slowly the long ago years came back in memory.

"Me Cynthia Ann," she said.

Mr. Parker took the long-lost Cynthia Ann home with him. But she was not happy and longed to return to the Indians, so her relatives agreed for her to return to the life she loved. Her oldest son, Quanah, became the chief of the tribe. A town in Texas is named in his honor.

And so ends the story of Cynthia Ann Parker, the best known little pioneer girl.*

A replica of Fort Parker was built in 1935 and is now a state park. The spring is still flowing.

Fort Parker is located near Groesbeck. A sign tells you where to turn off the highway.

Wouldn't you like to see the place where Cyn-

* There are minor differences in the accounts of the capture of Cynthia Ann. My great-great grandfather came to Limestone County a few years after the fall of Fort Parker. This is the story as my grandmother told it to me.

The Author

thia Ann and her playmates lived so many years ago?

MORE ABOUT TEXAN PIONEERS

If you wish to know more about Fort Parker State Park, write to the Sixth Grade in either Groesbeck or Mexia.

Here are some words familiar to every pioneer boy and girl. Do you know the meaning of each one?

spinning wheel
loom
cotton cards
coffee mill
flint
gourd dipper
slate and pencil
flat iron
trundle bed
ash hopper
shoe last
Webster's Blue Back Speller

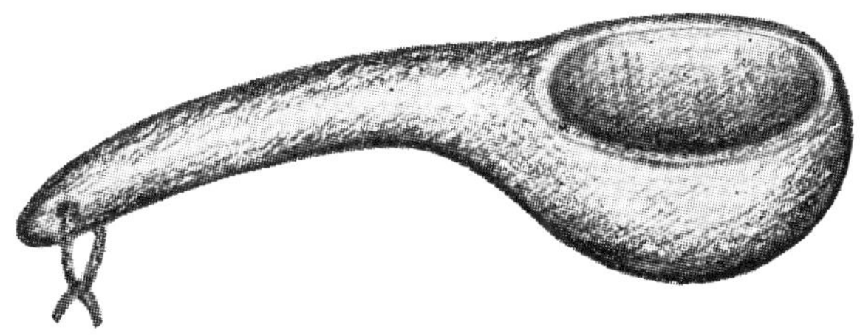

THE EARLY SCHOOLS IN TEXAS

The very first schools in our state were the Spanish missions. The priests were intelligent, patient men. Along with their other duties, they were good teachers.

The mission priests taught a few of their brighter students to read and write. But after the religious instruction was given, most of their day was spent teaching the Indians better ways of farming, how to care for livestock, and how to cook and sew. Schools where these practical skills are taught are called vocational schools. The Spanish missions were the first vocational schools in Texas.

Some of the Spanish townspeople in San Antonio, especially the families from the Canary Islands, were people of culture. They had a private school for the children. This was the first elementary school in the state.

Spelling lesson time.

Then came the years when the colonists arrived in great numbers. Some have the mistaken idea that most of the pioneers were ignorant and unschooled. On the contrary, many of them were college graduates; and many more were people of culture and refinement.

Stephen F. Austin, the Father of Texas, was a college graduate, an honor student, and an able writer.

Lamar, Father of Education in Texas, was a scholarly gentleman. He was author of several books and many poems.

Travis, commander of the Alamo, was a well educated man. He was a schoolteacher, and later studied law.

Fannin, commander at Goliad, was a West Point man.

Erath, one of the first captains of the Texas Rangers, had diplomas from two colleges.

Childress, author of the Texas Declaration of Independence, was a brilliant lawyer, well informed on the science of government.

Zavala, first Vice-President of Texas, was sent to the older and better (at that time) universities of Europe to complete his education. He was especially interested in fairness and freedom for all people. He wrote several books on this subject.

And so the list might go on and on. It has been truthfully said that the signers of the Texas Declaration of Independence were the best educated such group in the world.

But among the first children to be born here, many did grow up unschooled. Their parents were interested in education and did the best they could. But they could not give their children the advantages which they had had, for the simple reason that the schools were not here to attend.

Suppose you had been a child in Austin's colony or in East Texas. What kind of school would you have attended? What would you have studied? What games would you have played? Who would have been your teacher?

Let us see what a typical school was like more than a hundred years ago.

Schools were much less alike then than now. There were no grades and standard course of study. Every teacher taught whatever he thought the children should know and in whatever way seemed best to him.

Sometimes the school was in a home. Or,

often a man in the community would donate the land, and the fathers of the children of school age would build a one-room log house. This was the school building. The fathers also dug a well for water. Schools were usually held in summer when no heat was needed. But if the school were open in the winter, fathers cut wood for fuel. Sometimes the big boys cut the wood themselves. Always the children and the teacher built the fires and kept the building clean.

The furniture was not what you have today. The children sat on long split-log benches. A higher split-log in front of them was their desk. These logs were far from smooth. Oftentimes while the teacher was having some lesson, a younger child would cry out.

"Ouch!"

"What's the matter, Johnny?"

"I have a splinter in me, Miss Lois."

"Bring me the big needle, Johnny."

When the splinter was out, they went on with the lessons. It didn't take the teacher long to remove the splinter. Maybe that was because she had so much practice.

Getting books to study was one of the biggest problems. Those who had real school books were lucky indeed. Whatever books the children had at home they brought to school to study. Almost every family had a copy of Webster's Blue Back Speller; and this book was studied by every pupil in the school.

Spelling and simple arithmetic were studied by all "classes," for a good part of the day. In one teacher's diary she tells of taking her hat box apart and writing on this pasteboard the multiplication tables.

Paper was very scarce and high, but most children had a slate for doing sums.

A few persons and families had brought a fairly good home library to Texas with them. Stephen F. Austin had an excellent library. Usually the teachers themselves owned the books used in the school as a classroom library. Any book in the community could be used by the teacher, who in turn passed the information along to the pupils.

Since there were so few books, teachers often taught by rote. That is, they would spell a word or repeat a sentence, and the pupils would say it after them.

"B, A, ba," said the teacher.

"B, A, ba," answered the children.

"K, E, R, ker," said the teacher.

"K, E, R, ker," chorused the children.

"B, A, K, E, R, baker," said the teacher.

"B, A, K, E, R, baker," said the children together.

Or, "Columbus discovered America in 1492," said the teacher.

And all the class would say after him, "Columbus discovered America in 1492."

So you see all studying was done aloud. If someone passed the schoolhouse and there was much noise, he would say, "This is a good school. All the boys and girls are studying and learning."

Nobody had even thought of a school lunchroom at that time. The pupils brought their lunches with them, in a dinner pail. Since the whole school had lunch at the same time, members of the same family often carried their lunch together. In that case, the dinner pail was a big bucket!

On the playground, groups gathered as they liked and played games of their own choice, just so long as there were safety and fair treatment for all.

The little girls played dolls. You should have seen their playhouses! Shelves were made by putting a board between two trees. Leaves were swept into a corner for a bed. Sometimes there were several "houses," kept by as many "families," with "visiting" back and forth.

Stiff-starch was a favorite game of the girls, too. The boys played ball, but not the girls. And everybody played Mumble-peg in the spring.

Wolf-over-the-River, Ante-over, Hide-and-Seek, Hop-Scotch, and Whip-Cracker were other games played by pioneer children.

The early schools, like the early churches, were the center of community life. All week the children came for their lessons. But Friday afternoon was a social occasion for the whole community.

Very often there was a Literary Club sponsored by the teacher. Unlike your school clubs, grown-ups as well as boys and girls belonged. Fathers, mothers, young people, and children took part on the same program.

There might be a play, poems, a debate, or recitations with funny parts that made the audience laugh. Sometimes on Friday or Saturday night they had box suppers, ice-cream suppers, musicals, or spelling bees. There were no movies, radios, or cars then. But the pioneers in Texas did not mope around—no, not they.

Some people think they had a better time than some of us do now.

And in the midst of this community life was the teacher.

There were few children in the school, so the teacher knew not only the pupils but their families as well. He, or she, was frequently invited to their homes for dinner or to spend the night. The pioneers counted it an honor to have the teacher and the minister as a guest.

In communities where there was no church building, church services were held in the schoolhouse. If there were no minister, oftentimes the teacher directed the community Sunday School.

You have seen how the men of the neighborhood could work together and build a school building, such as they had, in a few days. But finding a teacher was not so easy.

Sometimes no teacher could be found at all, and each mother taught her own children. Or, one person in the community who liked to teach and could do it well would teach other children, too, for a small tuition.

If a group of families moved here together, they sometimes brought a teacher with them. Very, very often the minister was also the schoolteacher. There were as many men teachers as women, and perhaps more. Since there were few pupils and only one teacher, that meant that men often taught the youngest children to read.

And yet, though they were few in number, there were some very fine teachers in the early days. Every boy and girl in our state should know who some of them were and what they did.

Stephen F. Austin himself never taught, but he was a great friend of education. He was a learned man, and over and over again he urged the parents in his colony to send their children to school. There were no free schools, so tuition must be paid for each child. Money was scarce, and sometimes paying this tuition meant that both children and their parents had to give up other things. But Austin always said an education was worth the work and sacrifice.

Austin tried to get teachers to come to his colony. He succeeded in getting the Mexican government to pass a law that public schools should be established in Texas. These schools were never built; and this was one of the reasons given for declaring Texas free from Mexico.

Josiah Wilbarger, for whom Wilbarger County is named, taught a school at Matagorda.

He was scalped by the Indians and left for dead. He recovered, and lived eleven years; but his scalp never grew entirely over his skull.

Gail Borden, the inventor of condensed milk, was a pioneer teacher of our state.

Henry Smith, the provisional governor of Texas, opened a school here in the early days.

The most interesting pioneer teacher was Thomas Jefferson Pilgrim. His very name makes us believe that his parents valued knowledge and learning, for Thomas Jefferson was one of the greatest friends of education America ever had.

Thomas J. Pilgrim arrived in Texas on Christmas Day, 1828.

"Merry Christmas, Mr. Pilgrim, and welcome to our colony," said Austin.

"Merry Christmas to you, Mr. Austin. This country is beautiful. What is that hanging from the trees?"

"These are live oak trees, Mr. Pilgrim. We call this growth Spanish moss."

"I've never seen it before. We have nothing like it in Connecticut," said Mr. Pilgrim.

"We are glad to have a teacher in this community. The children are so unused to study that they may be mischievous," continued Austin.

"They will work in my school, Mr. Austin. I love boys and girls but they must study and learn. I will have no monkey-shines."

Right away the school was started. Sunday came.

"Why aren't these children in Sunday School?" asked the new teacher.

When he learned that they had no Sunday School, he said he would start one. And he did.

The first Sunday School in Texas was organized in Austin's colony by a schoolteacher, Mr. Thomas J. Pilgrim.

Mr. Pilgrim taught school here for almost fifty years. Many of his pupils became leaders in our state.

One of his students, after he was grown-up and a famous judge, said that Mr. Thomas J. Pilgrim was "the best teacher in Texas and one of the best men in the world."

M. B. Lamar is called the Father of Education in Texas.

Two years after the battle of San Jacinto, Lamar was elected president of the Republic of Texas. The very first thing he asked Congress to do was to set aside state lands to support free public schools and to plan a state school system. This was done, though the schools were not actually started until about fifteen years later.

Our schools today are benefited by the wise, kindly foresight of M. B. Lamar.

After the Civil War, southern schools were closed or poorly taught. They were reorganized under the leadership of O. M. Roberts.

Many schools today are named for M. B. Lamar and O. M. Roberts.

The wealthier families sent their sons and daughters to colleges in the United States. But those parents who wanted their children to go to college but could not afford to send them so far away began to work toward establishing colleges in Texas.

The first college in the state was Rutersville College, near La Grange. Baylor University, well known to all of us, was founded more than a century ago.

Early-day Texas was a land of homes, schools, and churches. Almost before the pioneer home was completed the church and school were begun.

The pioneer teachers were constantly on the move. They would teach two months one place, and move on to the next community to conduct a brief school there.

Were these pioneer teachers "Dreamers on Horseback"? Do you think they ever dreamed of schools with many beautiful books, of buildings well heated and well lighted, and of better educational opportunities for every boy and girl in Texas?

Did they, along with many others, work to make this dream come true for you?

HISTORICAL REVIEW

No doubt you know incidents and stories of the pioneer days that have never been put into a book. Perhaps some older person in your family has told you of some experience of one of your forefathers.

Why not make a book of your own? Let all who wish to do so write a story. Other members of the group will prepare the book cover in art class.

Some of you may write a poem. Many books have both stories and poems.

This poem was written by Patricia May Gallagher, a pupil in the Seventh Grade, at Dallas.

BLUEBONNETS

Bluebonnets waiting so gay and so blue,
Standing all straight in the sun,
Waiting on hillside for me and for you,
Saying, "See my bluebonnets! Do come!"

I love these wee Texas bonnets I spy,
They are our state flower, you see,
Stretching away, like a patch of blue sky,
On the hillside for you and for me.

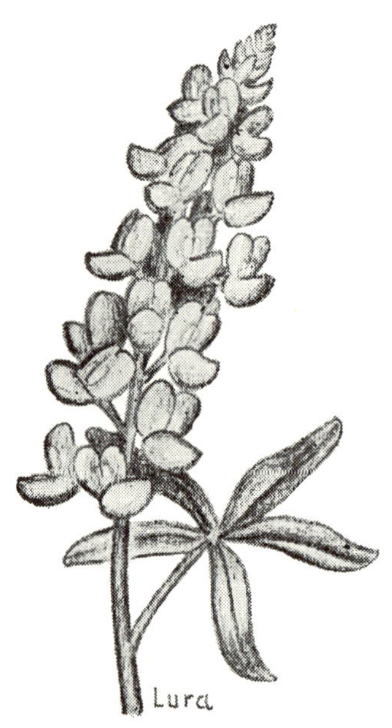

CHURCHES OF THE EARLY DAYS

The church is always the center of community life. With the pioneers, sometimes a little homesick for old friends and former homes and facing constant danger and trial, the church played an important role in their lives.

Both Spain and France are Catholic nations. Since they were the first to come to Texas, the first religious services in the state were Catholic. The earliest church in the state was in La Salle's colony, in the chapel within his fort. Several years ago an iron cross was found on the site of La Salle's colony. It is believed to have been used by these Frenchmen almost three hundred years ago. The cross is now above the entrance to a church in Port Lavaca. If you live in that part of the state, no doubt you have seen it there.

Next came the Spanish priests. In the story of Mission San Jose, you have learned of their work in Texas. Perhaps you will wish to reread "The Queen of the Missions" now.

Although the good Franciscan fathers labored in Texas for many years, their work was never as successful here as in California, the other state where a chain of missions was built. For one thing, the Indians were more savage here. And, too, the distances were greater.

Some have said that the work of these missionaries to the Indians was a failure. On the contrary, it is impossible to measure the benefits. Without the kindly influence of these padres (pä′ drās), Texas might not have become a civilized land of happy homes for many, many years later.

These priests made maps of Texas. In their reports and mission records, they wrote of the life of the Indians. Much that we know now about early Indian life in our state we have learned from the writings of the Franciscan fathers.

The priests also named many mountains and rivers in our state. Very likely you live near some place named by them.

Father Massanet (mä′sä nā′) and Father Margil (mär hēl′) worked faithfully for many years. Every Texan should know their names.

Sunday School of pioneer days.

Then came the colonists to make their homes here.

Mexico was a Catholic nation. Following the example of Spain, she made membership in the Catholic church one of the requirements for obtaining land. However, the rule was never enforced. Seguin (sā gēn′), an official of the Mexican government, stated that membership in good standing in any church was acceptable. So, you can see that an effort was made to choose good colonists. On the whole, they were honest, hard-working, and religious.

(Note: You will remember that this same Seguin joined the Texans in the war for independence. He fought in the battle of San Jacinto. The town of Seguin was named for him.)

Not all officials of the Mexican government were as liberal as Seguin, however. Since those attending Protestant services *could* be—though seldom were—punished by law, most of the services before Texas won her independence were quiet gatherings in the homes.

All churches other than Jewish synagogues (sĭn′ȧ gŏgs) and the Catholic church are called Protestant churches. They conduct their services somewhat alike and have many beliefs in common. Perhaps you know that already.

Of the Protestant churches, we cannot be sure which is the very oldest one in Texas. Several were established in different parts of the state at about the same time. All are more than a hundred years old, and all have done a wonderful work in the development of the state.

About the time that Austin came to Texas, William Stevenson, a circuit (traveling) preacher, started a Sunday School near the Red River, in what is now Red River County. At that time, the boundaries had not been made definite; and this area was believed to be a part of Arkansas. No church building was ever erected. In summer the members gathered under the shade of the large trees and in winter they met in someone's home.

Because there were no good roads, persons living near a river often traveled in canoes. If you visit that neighborhood on the Red River today, residents will point out to you an old tree where these pioneers anchored their boats while they attended church or Sunday School.

Another Sunday School of the early days was organized by Mr. Thomas J. Pilgrim in Austin's colony. It, too, was held either in the home of one of the members or out-of-doors.

The grandfather of Cynthia Ann Parker organized a church in East Texas, near Elkhart. This is believed to be the oldest Protestant Church in the state. Rev. Daniel Parker was a very religious man. When the wagon train of the Parker families and their friends was coming to Texas from Illinois, they did not travel on Sunday. Wherever they were, they stopped and had services.

Two early churches were built at Washington-on-the-Brazos.

Churches were built in the early days at San Augustine and Nacogdoches.

In Sabine County, near a ferry on the Sabine River, was a church named McMahan's Chapel. Many camp meetings were held there in the time when Texas was a republic.

Two years before the battle of San Jacinto, a man stood under a large elm tree in Nacogdoches. Many soldiers had passed this way, both Spanish and French. But today a soldier of another sort stood there.

The man was Rev. Henry Stephenson, an early-day minister.

The congregation was a motley group. There were a dozen or more frontiersmen, bronzed and bearded, with guns in hand. There were a few Mexican soldiers, several Mexican women with bright shawls over their heads, and a half-dozen wide-eyed Mexican children. On the outer edge of the group stood some Indians.

One who was there that day said that Stephenson faced the group with a small book in his hand. His eyes shone with a soft light, and his voice was kindly and earnest.

At the close of the sermon, they sang a hymn. Then they pressed forward to tell Rev. Stephenson good-by. He spoke encouraging words to them, promised to come back, and rode into the lonely forest. In his saddle bags were a Bible and a few hymn books. He was on his way to preach in the far outposts of Texas.

Fortunately, someone was so impressed with this sermon that he wrote down the date and incidents. For this reason we know the name of the preacher, the time, and the place. But this sermon was typical of many others not recorded, preached by these traveling preachers in the early days.

In 1835, a Protestant church was organized in Bastrop, Texas. Because the bylaws required ten members and there were only nine white people of this faith, they added the name of a negro slave. Celia was a faithful member until her death.

Less than a year before Travis died in the Alamo, he wrote a letter to a church magazine. His plea was for more ministers to come to Texas. In the letter he said that the people of Texas were shrewd and intelligent; therefore, to do any good, a preacher must be respectable and talented. Travis closed his letter in this way: "In sending your heralds to the four corners of the earth, remember Texas."

The plea was answered. At least two ministers came. At Caney Creek Camp Ground, in Austin County, a camp meeting was held. Since the people lived long distances from each other and the mode of travel was slow, the people came and camped for a series of meetings. For this camp meeting at Caney Creek in late summer of 1835, William B. Travis promised the preachers protection. Always, of course, these pioneers must be on guard against Indians. And there was a sprinkling of rough characters who did sometimes "break up the meeting."

The earliest colleges in the state were built by churches. One of these, Baylor University, is still operating. It has grown from a small beginning more than a hundred years ago to one of the greatest universities in the nation.

Rev. Z. N. Morrell, a preacher who took part

in the famous Plum Creek fight with the Comanches, wrote an account of his life. In the book he tells this interesting true story.

He preached at a schoolhouse, near Gonzales. The Indians were known to be on the warpath. Beside Morrell's Bible lay his gun, ready in case of attack. Men sat near each window and door with guns across their knees.

When the congregation was dismissed, war whoops were heard. All the people had to travel the same road the first part of the trip home. The preacher pulled his wagon, drawn by an ox-team, in the lead. The others fell in line behind him. One of the ladies suggested that they sing a hymn.

It was a beautiful moonlight night. Occasionally they got glimpses of Indians in the distance. Often their singing was almost drowned out by fierce war whoops.

But all those attending the service in the schoolhouse that night arrived home safely.

The next day they learned that a family who lived nearby, but who had not attended the meeting, was massacred.

At another time Morrell was traveling in Southwest Texas with a group of surveyors. In all, there were twelve men in the party. Morrell and one other man rode out together, on an errand taking them about thirty miles from camp. They came upon a lone Indian. Morrell's companion raised his gun to kill the Indian; but Morrell insisted that his life be spared, since their own lives were not in danger.

Late the next day they arrived at camp. They found the place surrounded by about forty hostile Indians.

By means of an interpreter, Morrell tried to convince the Indian Chief that they were friends.

The old chief then asked, "Were any of your men out hunting yesterday? Describe the horses you rode."

A young boy was brought forward. He identified Morrell and his companion as the ones he had seen the day before.

"You are our friends," said the chief. "You saved my boy's life."

Not only did the Indians leave without harming the surveying party, but they also returned the stolen property.

Kindness and mercy shown to a young Indian boy had saved all their lives.

One of the men in the Mier Expedition who drew one of the Black Beans was Major Dunham, a minister. He offered prayer for himself and his sixteen comrades before they were shot.

Rev. Andrew Jackson Potter is sometimes called "The Fighting Parson." For many years he was a Texas Ranger.

A Jew, Samuel Isaacs, was one of The Old Three Hundred with Austin. Others came to Texas afterward. The first synagogue was established in Houston in 1854. Even now Jewish centers of worship are found only in the large cities of the state. Though fewer in number, the Jews have made their own contribution to the state and worship in their synagogues among us.

We have seen how religious services were conducted in our state in the days of its early history. Let us think now of the churches your grandparents, or maybe great-grandparents, attended.

Oftentimes, when no minister was in the community, the neighbors would meet together to read Scripture and pray. Such a service was called a prayer meeting.

Sometimes the people in a neighborhood formed community churches. That meant that all faiths worshiped together. Where there were only fifteen or twenty people belonging to a half-dozen or more churches, they couldn't possibly build that many buildings. Nor were there enough people to need several churches. But they could build one church building and worship together. In some places in our state there are community churches today.

Pioneer Texans took pride in their hospitality. The minister was a welcome guest in every home. It was counted a great honor to have him visit for Sunday dinner or even stay overnight with the family.

Have you ever heard of a "Dinner-on-the-Ground"? My, how you would have liked being there!

A "Dinner-on-the-Ground" was religious service, banquet, music festival, and social occasion all in one.

The leading citizens of a community would decide on a date for the all-day meeting. Then news was spread, told from person to person. A blanket invitation was issued to everybody. All who came were welcome.

There were busy days in the community giving the dinner. First a preacher must be secured, the best that could be found. Then the best singers, or song leaders, must be invited personally. Additional song books must be borrowed from other communities. Long tables made of logs and lumber must be built. (The dinner was eaten on a table erected on the church grounds, hence the name.) All these things were done by the men.

The women, too, were very busy. The church must be dusted and decorated. A "Dinner-on-the-Ground" was held only in the spring or summer, so there were always many flowers in bloom.

And the food they cooked! Trunks were emptied and packed with all kinds of delicious food. From an old letter we have the following list of what one lady carried:

"We had all-day services with dinner-on-the-ground last Sunday. I baked a turkey, fried six chickens, baked two hams, baked six cakes, and ten pies. I carried two quarts of peach pickles and three quarts of cucumber pickles. I almost forgot to mention the things from my garden—lettuce, radishes, green beans, and corn.

"Margaret was there, too. You remember she married last year. She is a good cook and had several well-filled baskets. Everybody said her jam cake was the best cake there.

"Sophronia was there. I heard that she brought only three cakes. You know she always was stingy.

"People came for miles around but we had plenty of food."

At last the big day came. All who could wore

a new dress that day. On Sunday morning, the people assembled in the church and listened to a sermon.

Then came the feast! In some ways, being a pioneer child wasn't so bad, was it?

After dinner, everybody did what he liked best. The main event was the singing of hymns in the church. All the music lovers, especially, were there.

But little groups were gathered in the shade of the trees on the grounds, too. Perhaps they were old friends who had not seen each other for a long time. They just laughed and talked together.

Some of the children returned to the church to join the singers. Others played outside. And the youngest ones took their naps on a pallet brought along for that very purpose.

About four o'clock in the afternoon someone would tell all the groups it was time to dismiss. Everybody would come into the church and the minister would give the benediction. Then all the visitors would tell their hosts and hostesses how splendid it had all been, and everybody would go home.

Denton, Wilson, and Crane counties are named for pioneer preachers.

As these early-day preachers traveled long, weary miles to teach the people better ways of living, do you think they dreamed of beautiful church buildings, of regular and better religious services, of the people living happily and helpfully together? Is this the true meaning of the brotherhood of man under the Fatherhood of God?

Were thcsc pioneer preachers "Dreamers on Horseback"?

WORD STUDY

Benefits—Good results
Blanket invitation—An invitation which includes all, as a blanket covers all
Bronzed—Having a brown color; sunburned
Constant—Regular; all the time
Contrary—The opposite, as yes and no; "on the contrary" means "on the other hand"
Definite—Exact; fixed
Encouraging—Hopeful; helpful
Erected—Built
Former—Earlier; the one before
Hospitality—Kind and polite treatment of guests in one's home
Hostile—Unfriendly; warlike
Labored—Worked
Liberal—Open-minded; kind; not too strict

Massacred—Killed in a cruel manner or in great numbers
Motley—Mixed up
Obtain—To keep; to get
Padre—Spanish word meaning *father;* the Spanish priests were called padres.
Resident—One who lives in a place for some time
Talented—Mentally gifted; intelligent
Typical—Like many others in a group

Find these words in the story. Use these words in sentences of your own.

A SUGGESTED ACTIVITY

A Catholic house of worship is called a cathedral or parish church.

A Protestant house of worship is called a church.

A Jewish house of worship is called a synagogue.

Draw a picture of the one you attend.

An excellent new book is *One God—The Ways We Worship Him;* Florence Mary Fitch; Lothrop, Lee and Shepard Co., New York, N. Y. Do you know this book?

Perhaps your teacher will read parts of this book to the class. Some of you may become so interested that you will wish to read the entire book.

COME QUICK, DOC!

It was the middle of the night. There was a call at the doctor's gate. He roused himself from sleep to answer.

But there was nothing sleepy about the voice at the gate.

"Come quick, Doc! Mary Jane has an awful stomach ache. She's out of her head."

Dr. Hill knew Mary Jane. She was twelve years old. In the days when people knew very little about eating the right foods, and when modern refrigeration was unknown, acute indigestion was a common illness. Often the patient was delirious and dangerously ill.

In a very short time the two men, one middle-aged and the other very young, were riding as fast as they could over the wet, slippery road toward the little sick girl.

A heavy rain had fallen the day before. As they neared Big Creek, they could hear the roar of the water.

At the water's edge, the horses stopped dead still. Peering into the darkness, the men knew the reason why.

The bridge was out!

The men tried to urge the horses into the swirling water, but they would not go.

Mary Jane's big brother was almost frantic.

"She's mighty sick," he said.

"Don't worry, Bob," said the doctor. "I think I know a plan that will work."

With all his strength, Dr. Hill shoved his horse into the water. He jumped into the saddle as the water reached the animal's body.

"Good boy, Snip. Steady now."

Encouraged by his master's voice, Snip swam to the other side.

After the manner of horses, the second one followed Snip.

The men arrived at the farmer's home. Soon Mary Jane's pain was relieved. In a few days she was well and strong again.

Many doctors had calls in the night. Away out in West Texas a cowboy called at another young doctor's gate.

"Come quick, Doc! A cowboy at Mesquite Ranch is bleeding to death."

Mesquite Ranch was more than forty miles

"Come quick, Doc!"

away. No horse could run at full speed that far. Men had ridden ahead and had a fresh horse saddled and waiting every five miles.

Over and over again, the doctor leaped from foaming horse to one fresh and prancing, swinging his saddlebags behind him.

But could any man last that long?

He did. Eight times he changed horses. But he arrived in time, and the life of the cowboy was saved.

Dr. Crunk, lean and wiry and just out of medical school, made this heroic ride almost fifty years ago.

The pioneer doctor was an important member of the community. Strangely enough, his medical care of the people was more a public service than a means of livelihood. Although he cared for his patients faithfully and with the best skill known at that time, his practice did not make a living for the pioneer doctor. So, he was also farmer, or merchant, or innkeeper.

But the doctor was loved as a friend and civic leader. His advice was sought on all sorts of matters.

Where shall I send my son to school?

Shall I buy more land now, Doc?

We need a church in this community. Will you help us organize one and find a preacher?

Coming with Stephen F. Austin's Old Three Hundred was a doctor, Dr. Robert Andrews. He at once became Austin's closest friend. The two men made a trip to Mexico City on horseback together.

There were sixteen doctors in the Battle of San Jacinto. Dr. A. W. Ewing was Surgeon General, and Dr. Anson Jones was Assistant Surgeon General and Purveyor of the Army. It was Dr. Ewing who took charge of the treatment of Sam Houston's wounded leg.

When Santa Anna was brought before Sam Houston, they could not understand each other.

"We can't draw up terms of peace in a sign language!" boomed Sam Houston. "Search among the men until you find one who can speak both Spanish and English."

Soon the messengers returned.

"Sir, this is Dr. Nicholas La Badie. He can help you."

So it was that a doctor, a French Canadian by birth, acted as interpreter at San Jacinto.

Of all the pioneer doctors in Texas, Dr. Samuel Stivers was one of the most colorful and interesting characters. He settled in East Texas, where his patients included many Indians. Because he was six feet four inches tall the Indians called him Big Doctor.

During the Battle of San Jacinto, Sam Houston ordered the doctors to stay at the rear of the lines and care for the wounded. But Dr. Stivers, on his big gray Kentucky horse, kept dashing to the front. Santa Anna's men soon learned that he could wield a sword as well as a scalpel!

Three times Sam Houston sent Dr. Stivers word to go to the back of the line, but he disregarded the order. Then Houston, no doubt exasperated but without ill-will (for they were the best of friends) sent this message: "Stay in front, and I hope they shoot your head off!"

But they didn't. Dr. Stivers practiced for many years in Angelina County. Several descendants followed him in the profession.

Another interesting story is told about Dr. Stivers. His first thought after the Battle of San Jacinto was of his family. But he had no cause for worry. Hurrying home, he found all well. The Indian Chief had kept a guard around his home. The chief said to Mrs. Stivers, "Big Doctor help us; now we take care of you and little ones for Big Doctor."

Many physicians have made great contributions to Texas, but the two who perhaps did most for our state during the pioneer days are Dr. Charles Bellinger Stewart and Dr. Anson Jones.

Dr. Stewart attended the convention at Washington-on-the-Brazos and signed the Declaration of Independence. He designed our lone star flag. There are several stories about the origin of our state seal. One of them says that Dr. Stewart suggested the five-pointed star encircled by live oak and olive branches.

After the death of Stephen F. Austin, Dr. Stewart was appointed Secretary of State.

Dr. Anson Jones played an important part in the making of this state. He, too, fought in the Battle of San Jacinto. During Sam Houston's second term as President, Dr. Jones was Secretary of State.

When a young man, Dr. Jones had taught school. He was a valuable adviser to President Lamar in planning the public school system in Texas.

Dr. Jones was the last President of the Republic. To him belongs much credit for the annexation of Texas.

Jones County was named for him one year after his death. The county seat was named Anson.

Dr. Ashbel Smith is another who did much for our state. He was one of the organizers of the University of Texas and was a powerful influence in the early medical schools. Dr. Smith's library of about four thousand volumes is now a part of the University of Texas.

Dr. Anson Jones, Dr. Charles Stewart, and others served our state seventy-five and a hundred years ago. At that time calls were made almost altogether on horseback. The doctor carried his medicine with him in saddlebags. He often made long rides, sometimes as far as thirty, forty, or fifty miles.

Let us think now of what a doctor's life was like about fifty years ago.

The doctor still must keep a good saddle horse for long trips or traveling in a hurry, but he had a buggy, too. A few, especially those in larger cities, had cars.

If the doctor went in a buggy, his wife often put in heated bricks to keep his feet warm. Wherever he stopped to make a call, these bricks were re-heated.

Since there was no drug store nearby as we have today, the doctor carried his medicine with him. A medicine case was carried in the buggy as the saddlebags had been on horseback.

The doctors of those days had to contend with many superstitions, not all of which are gone today. For example, long after it was proved that the mosquito carried malaria, many persons believed that night air would cause this sickness; and they would not open their windows for ventilation. People used to crowd into small houses visiting the sick, keeping the patient from getting proper rest. It has taken years for people to learn that children should not be exposed needlessly to contagious childhood diseases.

Back in these times a doctor's horse was practically his partner. Sometimes he would be out in storms when it would be so dark he couldn't see his hand before his face. Then he would give his horse full rein, and the animal would pick his own way without harming himself or his rider.

Shackelford, Starr, Throckmorton, Jones, Hill, Archer, and Motley Counties are named for pioneer doctors. Dr. Motley was killed in the Battle of San Jacinto.

Were the pioneer doctors "Dreamers on Horseback"?

Surely they must have had great dreams as they rode long miles—dreams of an improved and populated country, dreams of better ways of healing the sick body. Some of their dreams have come true. And yet, some of the unknown in medical science is still to be explored, so our present day doctors are pioneers, too.

MAKING NEW WORDS

Medical science is always working to make new discoveries.

Now, let's make some new words. Shall we?

I. Make new words from these little words by putting them together to make longer words:

some thing how any for ever

II. Make new words by placing "un" or "be" before these words:

tie come afraid fore happy selfish

III. Make new words by adding "ing" or "ly" after these words:

show jump slow quick call glad

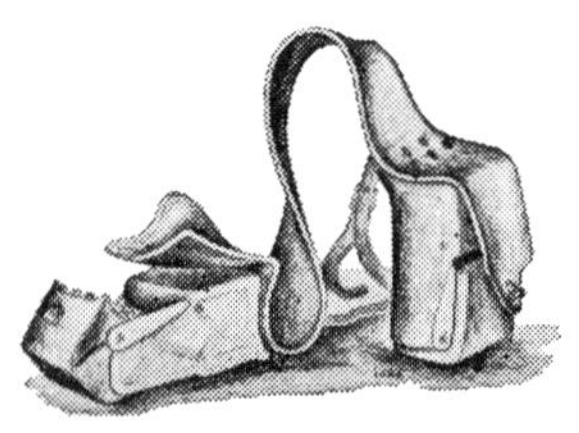

A SON OF TEXAS BECOMES GOVERNOR

It was March. At Mountain Home, comfortable plantation residence of Mr. and Mrs. Joseph Hogg, everyone was busy and happy. The faithful negro slaves plowed the fields and planted seeds. The large vegetable garden had long rows of tender young onions, potatoes, and radishes.

Mr. Hogg was the most successful lawyer in Rusk, Texas. Intelligent and lovable Mrs. Hogg presided in her home with the graciousness of a queen. Martha and Thomas were sent to the best private school at Rusk. Little Joseph would go to the same school when he was older. Today he was riding a stick horse up and down the garden rows as Mammy gathered fresh vegetables for dinner. Every now and then she called to him, warning him not to trample the potatoes standing prim and straight.

Mammy and little Joseph went back to the house.

"Land sakes, Mrs. Lucinda (Mrs. Hogg), just look at that redbud tree! Warm days like this, and the dogwoods will be popping out any time now. March has sure come in like a lamb!"

But March went out like a lion. A little later there was a storm—a bad one. And in the midst of the storm, on March 24, 1851, James Stephen Hogg was born.

Jim Hogg often mentioned that storm in later years. He said it was an omen for his life and Texas.

Jim's earliest years at Mountain Home were happy ones. He enjoyed long hikes with his older brothers through the tall pines. He went hunting and fishing. True enough, he was expected to bring home meat for the table. But do you not agree that such an errand was more pleasant than a trip to the grocery store?

East Texas in the fifties was busy and prosperous. The family life of the Hoggs was simple, but they had all the necessities and some of the luxuries. Food was plentiful and varied. Everyone on the plantation, from slave to master, was well clothed in garments woven on the place. Young Jim knew the security of

For three days they had only watermelon.

wealth and family honor. And early in life he learned from his kindly parents a strong sense of obligation of the strong toward the weak.

When Jim was seven, his father began taking him each morning in the family carriage to the private school in Rusk. There were no public schools then.

Boundary lines of Texas had been fixed when it became one of the states in the United States, six years before young Jim was born. But actually nearly all of the population of the state was in East Texas at that time. Dallas was only a small village. Fort Worth was a fort, with soldiers to protect stage-coach travelers from Indian raids. The land lying west of these outposts was unknown and dangerous.

But Jim heard much talk of these vast lands to the west. He heard his father and his friends speak of these millions and millions of acres of public land. The land was worth very little, they said. But some expressed their dreams and hopes for the future. Mr. Hogg, young Jim's father, even said that some day there would be a system of free public schools where *every* child, rich or poor, could receive an education. The others laughed at this and called it a pipe dream. Young Jim wondered about all these things, and first began to imagine a greater Texas.

Then came war between the North and South. Dark clouds were gathering over Texas, and over the peaceful boyhood of Jim Hogg.

His father died in the war. A year later his youngest brother, Richard, died of a contagious fever sweeping the country. A few weeks later his mother also died.

Martha, a young war widow, returned to Mountain Home. She and her brothers had a hard struggle, but they managed as well as their older neighbors.

"Those Hogg young ones have spunk," the neighbors said.

At last the war was over. Like many other Southern families, the Hoggs had seen their personal fortune dwindle and almost vanish. Four years before, they had been well-to-do. Now they were practically penniless.

Jim Hogg was sixteen years old. He had grown tall and large and strong. He was willing to work—and to work hard—at anything he could do.

But what could he do? He had had to stop

school and go to work when he was twelve. He was trained for no special work. He was just a poor farmer's boy, looking for a job.

The editor of the newspaper at Rusk gave Jim his first job. It was hard work and poor pay.

But Jim was so eager to be helpful and to learn that he soon became a favorite in the office. The editor let him read proof. As he read the editorials on the political condition of the country, he became interested for the first time in government.

This boy, without father or mother to advise him, was clever enough to know that he must have an education. He went back to school, paying for his board and lessons by chopping wood, milking cows, or doing any other needed chore.

When the school term was ended, Jim Hogg heard that they needed a printer in the new town of Cleburne. He and his friends thought he was going far west. He walked along sandy roads and over black prairies. Since he did not wish to wear out his precious shoes before he arrived, he walked barefoot.

The prairies were very different from the green pine forests he knew. Soon after he arrived in Cleburne, Jim became homesick. On his way home, in Waxahachie, a man who had known his father in the war gave him a lift in his oxteam freight wagon.

Jim had only twenty cents, but the teamster had provisions and was willing to share them.

"By gatlins!" he said. "Any son of General Hogg is a friend of mine from here to thunder."

But the first night out wild hogs ate their food, as they slept.

"By gatlins!" said the old man.

Jim offered his twenty cents. With it they bought three watermelons. For three days they had watermelon for breakfast, dinner, and supper.

Years later when Governor James Hogg would see a watermelon he would laugh and say, "By gatlins! This reminds me—"

Jim had worked in Rusk only a short time when he left to work on the newspaper at Quitman, the county seat of Wood County.

That fall Jim decided to try his hand at farming. The first year he was a sharecropper; the next year a tenant farmer. Here he learned what a hard row the farmer has to hoe. All his life James S. Hogg was very sympathetic toward the problems of the farmer and laborer.

Jim's next move was to Tyler, where he again worked on the newspaper. He pondered over the news in the type he set. New settlers were pouring into the state. The cattle industry was thriving on the lands in the west. Railroads were being built. Old and prosperous towns became smaller if the railroad missed them. New towns were built along the newly-laid lines.

Jim Hogg began to study law at night.

When he was twenty, Jim began the publication of his own newspaper at Longview. The next year, urged by his old friends to do so, he moved his newspaper to Quitman.

Though a young man, Jim had met many people and understood their problems. He had many friends.

When he was twenty-two, he was elected county judge. A year later he married lovely Miss Sallie Stinson of Quitman.

Never before or since has Texas known such a county judge. He was six-feet-two and weighed almost two hundred and fifty pounds. To make his face look older than his twenty-three years, he grew a goatee and sideburns.

When Hogg took office, the county debt was

$20,000. Thirty months later the debt was less than $1,000, and the taxes had been greatly reduced!

In 1876 James Hogg was admitted to the bar and opened his own law office in Quitman.

The year 1876 was an important year in Texas. In that year our present State Constitution was written.

Jim Hogg studied the Constitution, as it was being written, with keen interest. He said the best thing about it was the ease with which the people could change it. All his life he believed in the wisdom of the people. He believed that the will of the majority would always be the wisest and best thing to do. He thundered, in every speech he made, that it was dangerous and wrong for the government of the people to be run by a few men.

Then Hogg was elected county attorney of Wood County. Two years later he was made district attorney.

"Jim Hogg is fair and impartial," the people said. "We need more men like him."

Mr. and Mrs. Hogg now had a daughter, Ima, and three boys, William, Mike, and Tom. Their father knew he must think of saving money for their education. He moved to Tyler to engage in private practice of law. He did well from the start.

But Jim Hogg was unhappy and troubled. He saw injustices, which he knew had their roots in unfair laws. He saw the rich becoming richer and the poor becoming poorer. He knew this was not right. As no other man of his time, he knew the needs of the common man. His sympathies were with them—the farmer, the laborer, and the small business man—and he wanted very much to help them.

When Jim Hogg was thirty-five years old, he was elected Attorney-General of Texas. Sul Ross, the Ranger who rescued Cynthia Ann Parker, was governor.

Hogg was not the kind of man to "make a deal" with anybody. He did what was right and fair to all.

Because there was no government regulation of the railroads at that time there were many unfair practices. Rates were high. Service was poor. A rich man who did much shipping was charged low rates. Poor men were charged very high rates. Jim Hogg went to work to correct these wrongs.

The state had given land to the railroads.

This was right and best for all, for transportation was needed to build the new state. But some of the railroads had presented false claims for land. As attorney-general, Hogg sued and recovered an amount of land about equal to the state of Rhode Island.

Hogg said there should be a Railroad Commission.

A commission, like a committee, is made up of several persons. Jim Hogg always believed that people should work together in friendliness, and that what is decided by a group of people will be wiser than the decision of one man. That is part of what democracy means.

Less than a month after his thirty-ninth birthday, James S. Hogg announced his candidacy for governor.

He went back to his old home at Rusk. Nearby towns sent brass bands. People came from miles around. In the large crowd were men and women dressed in the latest fashion. And there were men in overalls and women in sun-bonnets, too.

Jim Hogg made a long and wonderful speech. He spoke of the storm in which he was born. He said Texas politics were in a storm, too. He promised that, if he were elected governor, he would create the Railroad Commission, lengthen the term of free schools, and pass certain other laws which would be for the welfare of all. He called these proposed improvements the "Hogg Code."

James Stephen Hogg was elected Governor of Texas. And he kept every promise he had made.

Hogg's inauguration was the first to take place in the newly completed capitol at Austin. Too, he was the first governor of our state who was a native born Texan.

Because Hogg worked for the best of *all* the people, he is spoken of even today as the *people's* Governor of Texas. Because of his large physical size, he was called Big Governor. You remember that he was six-feet-two, and when he was elected governor he weighed over three hundred and fifty pounds.

Big Governor had many friends, but none whose friendship he treasured more than the children who knew him. Boys and girls seemed to know right away that he was worthy of being trusted, and they liked him. And he liked them, too.

Governor Hogg served his state well. He caused to be passed several wise and just laws from which we benefit today. And yet, Hogg left the governor's office with less than fifty dollars in cash.

He opened a law office in Austin, and several years later moved to Houston. By hard work and good business judgment, he did build up a personal fortune before his death.

Big Governor knew he was very ill. He expressed this last wish to his family:

"I don't want any cold marble placed at the head of my grave. I want a soft-shelled Texas pecan tree planted there. The children will gather the nuts and plant them near their homes. Thus, in time, Texas soil will bring forth rich harvests of pecans."

Texas loved this man with the jolly smile and booming voice. Jim Hogg County is named for him. On the campus of the University of Texas stands a statue in his honor. The Jim Hogg State Park, near Rusk, is being developed now.

Big Governor was a big man: big in body, with a great, loving heart.

Some people say even today that he was the best governor Texas ever had. He was wise, and fair, and honest.

Perhaps some boy or girl who reads this story

will grow up to become that kind of governor of our state.

Texas needed Big Governor in his day. It needs good governors now. And it will need good governors when those who are children today are grown-up men and women.

CAN YOU TELL?

1. Why are there so many schools in Texas named for James Stephen Hogg?

2. One of Hogg's good friends who helped him set up the "Hogg Code" was John H. Reagan. Do you know a school named for him?

3. What does "in the fifties" mean?

4. What does "read proof" or "proofread" mean?

5. Have you a picture among your family photographs of someone wearing a goatee and sideburns? Perhaps your grandmother can help you.

6. What does "admitted to the bar" mean?

7. Why had not the governors who preceded Hogg been born in Texas?

8. Why do you think the pecan was made our state tree?

A BOY'S SONG

by

JAMES S. HOGG

Where the pools are bright and deep,
Where the gray trout lies asleep,
Up the river, and over the lea,
That's the way for Billy and me.

Where the blackbird sings the latest,
Where the hawthorne blooms the sweetest,
Where the nestlings chirp and flee,
That's the way for Billy and me.

Where the mowers mow the cleanest,
Where the hay lies thick and greenest;
There to trace the homeward bee,
That's the way for Billy and me.

Where the hazel bank is steepest,
Where the shadow falls the deepest,

Where the clustering nuts fall free,
That's the way for Billy and me.

Can you guess who Billy was?
Do you enjoy going on an outing with your father?

NOTE TO READERS:

To fully understand both History and Geography we must study them at the same time.

Do not begin the chapters, "Stories of Texas Towns" and "Stories of Texas Counties," until you have a large map of Texas at hand. See that you have a map which shows both the towns and the counties.

Find every town and county that you read about on the map.

STORIES OF TEXAS TOWNS

As you have learned from other stories in this book, many people from many lands came to make their homes in Texas. They began coming soon after Cabaza de Vaca (kä bā′sä dā vä kä) told his tall tales, and they have not ceased at the present time. They came by covered wagon and flatboat, by steamer, and on slow, puffing trains of the early days. The land was young, and so were the people who came to inhabit it. Their lives read like story books. They have left a story for us in every town in Texas. It is not possible to tell of them all here. However, we shall tell the stories of a few you will read about in Texas History.

Perhaps you will become so interested you will wish to find out the stories of other towns, too.

SAN ANTONIO

San Antonio is the oldest of all the large cities in our state. It was founded as a mission by the good Spanish priests who came here to civilize the Indians. Five beautiful missions still stand in or near San Antonio. For this reason it is called the Mission City.

The colonies of Spain had three parts—the mission, the fort, and the village. The first mission was called San Antonio de Valero, the fort was known as San Antonio de Bexar (bā'här), while the village was first named San Fernando in honor of Fernando III, King of Spain. All three names are found there today. San Antonio is the name of the city and Bexar is the name of the county. In the heart of the city there is a beautiful old church which bears the name San Fernando.

Have you ever visited Mission San Antonio? Perhaps so; it is better known by another name. Only the chapel stands today, and it is called the Alamo from the cottonwood trees nearby. *Alamo* is the Spanish word for *cottonwood.*

In East Texas the missions were built of logs from the great trees in the forest all around them. But at San Antonio there were no pine

trees. From necessity the missions there were built of stone. No doubt the Spanish and Indian workers complained about hauling those heavy stones long, weary miles. And yet, it is fortunate for us that the missions there were built in this manner. Nothing remains of the East Texas missions, but the beautiful old buildings at San Antonio are much the same today as when the Indians and Spanish priests worshiped there so many years ago.

In the early days the Spanish government realized that San Antonio would become an important city some day. They sent sixteen families from the Canary Islands. Some of their descendants still live in this city, some of them on grants of land their forefathers received from the Spanish king.

When Mexico won its independence from Spain, and Texas was under the rule of the new nation of Mexico, San Antonio continued to be the seat of government. Perhaps you have seen the Governor's Palace. If not, you will wish to do so when you visit in this city.

Because there is sunshine almost the year round, San Antonio is sometimes called the "City of Sunshine." Flowers bloom in the yards even at Christmas time.

San Antonio was founded with a fort, and it is still a military city, being the largest military training center in the nation.

The beautiful San Antonio River winds its way through the city. Would you like to pretend that you are in Venice and ride through the city in a boat? You can.

This city has many modern buildings, too. One of the most interesting of these is the Municipal Auditorium.

San Antonio was founded by the Spanish in the mission period, and still retains its Spanish influence. It is a city with an atmosphere all its own. Texas is proud of its oldest and most unique city.

AUSTIN

Austin is the capital city of our state. It is located on the Colorado River, among green rolling mountains.

The first capital of Texas, after the Anglo-Americans came, was San Felipe de Austin. Other capital cities were Washington-on-the-Brazos, Columbus, and Houston.

In 1839 President Lamar appointed a group of men to choose the most desirable and beautiful spot in Texas for a capital.

They traveled here and they traveled there. They saw many beautiful sites. And then they came to a little village called Waterloo on the Colorado River.

These men saw the broad Colorado River flowing toward the Gulf. They saw the violet shadows on the mountains. They saw the fertile land rolling toward the south.

"This place is very beautiful," said one.

"And it is located in the center of the state's population," said another.

Perhaps someone remembered to say, "This is the spot Stephen F. Austin chose as the most beautiful spot in Texas." At any rate, Austin did plan to make his home there some day.

So the people chose the present site for the capital of Texas. They changed the name of the village from Waterloo to Austin. The capital city was named in honor of the Father of Texas, who had recently died while serving the land he loved.

One of the historic homes you will wish to see in Austin is the Old French Embassy. It is the only building ever erected by a foreign country on Texas soil. It was built for the home of the French Ambassador when Texas was a Republic.

The Governor's Mansion is of interest to all Texans. Perhaps some boy or girl who reads this book will some day live in it.

The Mansion was built in 1855 when E. M. Pease was governor. A group of men had selected another site, but Mrs. Pease insisted that the Governor's Mansion be built at its present location. We are glad the governor's wife did speak up, for she chose the better of the two sites.

When the stately mansion was completed, a purchaser was sent to New York to buy appropriate furniture and carpets.

This home stands today, with but slight change and addition, still beautiful and comfortable. Many of the pieces of furniture have historic interest. All visitors wish to see Austin's desk and Houston's bed.

When we visit Austin for the first time, the very first place we wish to see is the State Capitol. The great building has a dome rising more than three hundred feet, on which stands the Goddess of Liberty holding aloft the Lone Star. It is built in the form of a Greek cross. Our capitol is of red granite brought from Burnet County. It was paid for by a large grant of land in the Texas Panhandle. This land became the famous XIT Ranch, which at one time was made up of all or part of ten counties. Headquarters for this ranch today are in Deaf Smith County.

In Austin is the University of Texas. This is one of the largest and best universities in the nation.

Truly, Texas has a capital city of which Texans can be justly proud.

HOUSTON

Houston is the largest city in our state. It is often called the Magnolia City.

Houston was founded soon after the Battle of San Jacinto. It was named in honor of Sam Houston, who was in command of the Texan army.

General Houston had hopes that the city named in his honor would be the capital of Texas. While he was President of the Republic, it was made the seat of the government. But the people later chose Austin as the capital.

Harrisburg, an old Texas town often mentioned in Texas History, is now a part of the city of Houston.

San Jacinto Battlefield, now a State Park, is near Houston, between that city and Galveston.

Rice Institute is the largest privately endowed university in Texas. Baylor Medical School is located at Houston.

The city of Houston is an industrial and shipping center. Large ships come and go through the man-made Ship Channel, which connects with the Gulf of Mexico.

The landscape is flat and level. But one visiting in Houston looks up, not to see hillsides, but the tops of giant trees. There are tall pines and fragrant magnolias all around.

Houston is rightly called the Magnolia City.

DALLAS

Dallas is on the Trinity River, in northeast Texas, and in the most densely populated part of the state.

The first settler in Dallas was John Neely Bryan. A replica of his log cabin may be seen on the lawn of the county courthouse. Mr. Bryan was a great admirer of George M. Dallas, one of the Vice-Presidents of the United States, so he named the village he founded in his honor. This small village has become the city of Dallas.

Dallas is a "fashionable lady" kind of city. She looks more to the future than to the past.

Dallas is a fashion center and boasts that its ladies are the prettiest in the world.

It is a cultural center, taking great pride in its Symphony Orchestra, Art Museum, Museum of Dallas Historical Society, and its book stores.

Southern Methodist University, Hockaday School, and Southwestern Medical College are located in Dallas.

The old French colony, La Reunion, was

founded near Dallas a few years after Texas was annexed to the United States. The descendants of some of these French, Swiss, and Belgian colonists still live in Dallas.

Have you ever attended the Dallas Fair? Did you have a good time? Dallas takes great pride in having the largest State Fair in the world.

The rest of the year Dallas is a sedate lady. But during Fair Time this city is a tomboy and has a jolly good time!

FORT WORTH

Three years after Texas became a state, a fort was established on the Trinity River. It was named in honor of General William Jennings Worth, an army officer. This fort was to furnish protection from Indian raids, mostly the Comanches who swooped down from the Panhandle and West Texas. A town grew up around the fort, and has become the city of Fort Worth.

For many years after Fort Worth was settled, few people lived north and west of there. These were the days of the overland stagecoach. There was a stagecoach line between Fort Worth and Phoenix, Arizona. Outlaws and Indians often robbed and sometimes killed the passengers. Military protection was provided, Fort Worth being headquarters for the soldiers and scouts sent out along the route.

Fort Worth became a gateway city. It is one of the foremost stock markets of the nation. Large packing plants are located there. It is also a distributing point for oil field supplies.

The Fat Stock Show, held each year, besides being an exposition for stockmen, has a world championship rodeo.

Have you attended this rodeo? Were you reminded of earlier and wilder days in Texas?

GALVESTON

Galveston is called the Oleander City. The oleanders, both pink and white, line all the streets. In this mild climate, they are in bloom most of the year.

Galveston Island, and the city, are named for Bernardo de Galvez (ber när′dō dā gäl-vās), a Spanish military officer. Remains of these old Spanish forts can be seen today, not many miles from the modern military forts of the United States Army.

Galveston is the location of the oldest historical record of our state. It was here that Cabeza de Vaca (kä bā'sä dā vä'kä) landed more than four hundred years ago. Here he saw the tall Karankawa (kă răng'kä wä) Indians.

Jean Lafitte (zhän lä fēt'), the French pirate, once had his headquarters on Galveston Island.

Just across the bay, on a peninsula of the mainland, is Bolivar Point. It was here that Mrs. James Long, the Mother of Texas, waited in vain for her husband's return.

Years ago, in 1900, a hurricane almost destroyed Galveston. To make sure that this never happens again, a concrete sea wall was built along three miles of the waterfront. The surface of the city behind the wall was then raised by filling in with sand and earth. The exposed side of the sea wall is protected by granite blocks brought from Burnet County.

During the emergency after the storm, a new form of city government was set up. It is called the Commission Form. Many cities in Texas and other states now have this form of government.

The customs office here is one of the largest in the nation.

The University of Texas College of Medicine, with its medical center, is located here.

To most of us, Galveston means, first of all, a pleasure resort. Have you ever spent a vacation in Galveston? Did you have a good time?

EL PASO

El Paso was founded and named by the Spanish. Its full name was El Paso del Norte (āl pä′so dĕl nor′tā), meaning "The Pass of the North." For many, many years before the Pilgrims landed in America, Spanish explorers came up from Mexico into the lands occupied by the more civilized Pueblo Indians. The only break in the mountain chain is here, so El Paso was on the route of every bold adventurer.

The oldest town in the state is Ysleta (ēs lā′tȧ), near El Paso. Here a mission was founded by the Franciscan priests two years before La Salle landed at Matagorda Bay. The Indians at Ysleta readily accepted the missionaries' teachings. The church still stands; and a few Indians of the original tribe still live there, though they are fast losing identity as pure Indians.

The mission built at El Paso del Norte was located on the southern bank of the Rio Grande, so is now just over the line in Mexico. It is a very beautiful church, and is used today as a place of worship.

Many years ago the king of Spain established a fort at El Paso. Today the United States Army has a large fort there.

Many old Spanish customs are still found in El Paso. For instance, many windows and doors are painted blue. There is an old legend which says that no evil will cross a threshold painted the blue of the Blessed Virgin Mary.

Cabeza de Vaca, Coronado, and many others of these long ago days passed through El Paso. The stagecoach lines going west went through this mountain pass. The old cattle trails of this area used The Pass of the North. Today a transcontinental highway goes through El Paso.

Today, as yesterday, we cross the mountains of the Mexican border at El Paso del Norte.

WACO

Waco, built on both banks of the Brazos River, is sometimes called the "Queen of the Brazos." Since it is in almost the geographical center of the state, it is also sometimes called the "Hub City."

The city takes its name from a tribe of Indians,

now extinct. An early explorer wrote this description of the village:

"All around the village were corn fields and pumpkins and melons. The wigwams were built in rows and had an air of neatness and regularity about them I have never seen before in an Indian village. They were well provided with cured venison and buffalo meat."

Later a trading post was opened at the village.

The town of Waco was laid out by one of the Texas Rangers, George B. Erath. The first lots sold for five dollars each.

Crossing the swift Brazos was a problem before good bridges were built. Another Ranger, Captain Sul Ross, operated a ferry across the river and settlers began to come in.

The oldest university in the state, Baylor, is located at Waco.

AMARILLO

The first white men to see the treeless prairies of the most northern part of Texas were Coronado and his men in their knighthood finery, mounted upon prancing horses. While crossing the plains, they set up signposts by driving wooden stakes into the ground. Since then this part of Texas has been called Llano Estacado (yä′nō ās′tä kä′thō) or the Staked Plains.

Because the narrow, northern part of Texas extends like a handle, while the rest of the state widens like an odd-shaped pan, this part of Texas is generally known as the Panhandle.

The largest city in the Panhandle is Amarillo.

Amarillo is the Spanish word for yellow. Some say that the name refers to the reddish-yellow soil. Some say that the name was chosen from the coloring of the Palo Duro Canyon not many miles away. While others believe that someone saw the whole countryside covered with yellow wild flowers and exclaimed "Amarillo!"

Soon after the War between the States, the Legislature laid out and named fifty-four counties in the Panhandle. Amarillo is in Potter County, named in honor of Robert Potter, who signed the Texas Declaration of Independence.

Colonel Charles Goodnight is sometimes called the "Father of the Texas Panhandle." He went there when that section was almost a deserted plain and became one of the most famous ranchers of the West.

There was a time when Amarillo was a small town, a gathering place for cowboys on a Saturday night rampage. But today it is a growing modern city.

THE LITTLE TOWNS OF TEXAS

The little towns of Texas
  That nestle on her plains,
That gather close the inland roads,
  The homing trails and lanes;
The little towns of Texas
  That sleep the whole night long,
Cooled by a scented southern breeze,
  Lulled by its drowsy song!

The little towns of Texas
  Will ever seem to me
Like stars that light a prairie sky
  Or isles that dot a sea;
Like beads that sparkle here and there
  On Texas' flowered gown,
Like figures on its rich brocade
  Of purple, green, and brown.

The little towns of Texas
  Seen through the prairie haze,
How fair, how fresh, and free they lie
  Beneath the golden days!

Not crowded in deep valleys,
  Not buried in tall trees,
But open to the sun, the rain,
  The starlight, and the breeze!

The little towns of Texas,
  What pretty names they bear!
There's Echo, Garland, Crystal Springs,
  Arcadia, Dawn, and Dare!
There's Ingleside, and Prairie Home,
  And Bells, and Rising Star!
God keep them childlike, restful, clean,
  Pure as the prairies are!

—Clyde Walton Hill

NACOGDOCHES

Two years before San Antonio was founded, a mission was built at Nacogdoches. The name is that of the friendly tribe of Indians for whom it was built. They were one of the tribes in the Tejas Confederacy.

As in all of the Spanish missions, the village had three parts. There was the church, where the priests taught the Indians. There was the fort, with soldiers to protect the settlement from Indians on the warpath. And there was the community of families, the fathers of whom took care of the civil needs of them all. Some of these fathers were builders, others were farmers, while a few had shops and stores.

In Europe, Spain and France were at war. The colonies in America took up the quarrel. The French from nearby Louisiana did a rather foolish thing. They came against the people of Nacogdoches, who had done them no harm, and drove them from their homes. The Spaniards fled to San Antonio for protection.

But the settlers from Nacogdoches were not happy in San Antonio, although they were given land. The Spanish Vice-Roy in Mexico City could not understand this.

Wasn't the land at San Antonio fertile?

Yes, it was very good land but so was that at Nacogdoches, the colonists said.

Wasn't this a beautiful country?

The mesquites and live oaks were very beautiful indeed, but they missed the tall pines and bright holly.

It wasn't that there was *anything* wrong with San Antonio. But Nacogdoches was their *home,* and they loved it.

At last Antonio Gil Ybarbo (ăn tō′nĭ ō hēl ē bär′bō) said, soldiers or no soldiers, he was going home. He would protect his family himself. Others said they would do the same and went with him. So they returned to their old home and began the rebuilding of Nacogdoches.

Gil Ybarbo brought a few cattle with him. They thrived on the fine grass, and became one of the earliest ranch herds in the state.

Nacogdoches grew rapidly during the days of early colonization. Families coming in from the "Old States" crossed the Sabine and reached Nacogdoches. They were weary from their long, hard journey. After all, this was Texas. Why not stay here? And many of them did.

Nacogdoches is the oldest Anglo-American town in the state. When you go there you will wish to see the Old Stone Fort, one of the oldest Protestant churches in the state, and the college named for the Father of Texas.

Two other towns in East Texas mentioned in Texas History are Crockett and San Augustine.

The very first mission was built near Crockett. It was named Mission San Francisco de los Tejas. The Spaniards who built this mission called the country The Land of the Tejas. Later the spelling was slightly changed, and the land was called Texas.

There is a state park today on the site of this oldest mission in our state.

Crockett is named for Davy Crockett, hero of the Alamo. You will enjoy other stories about him. Many books have stories about David Crockett, so you can easily find them.

San Augustine, too, is one of the oldest towns in the state. There you will see large, beautiful homes more than a hundred years old.

SAN FELIPE DE AUSTIN

San Felipe de Austin, a small village in Austin County, is remembered and honored for what happened there in the early days of Texas. Both the town and the county are named for Stephen F. Austin, the Father of Texas.

Austin and his father's good friend, Baron de Bastrop, laid out the town. Most of The Old Three Hundred settled here. The town was the capital of Austin's colony, which made it the very heart of Texas.

Here several important conventions were held.

Here Sam Houston and James Bowie met and had Christmas dinner together.

Here the first book and newspaper in Texas were published.

Here Austin gave his wise and kindly advice.

The town of San Felipe de Austin is mentioned over and over again in Texas History. If you visit this town, try to picture how it must have looked when Austin, Houston, and so many others worked and planned to build your state.

GOLIAD

Goliad is one of the oldest towns in the state. You will remember that for many years Spanish settlements at Nacogdoches, San Antonio, and Goliad were the only ones in Texas. Only they and the Indians were here.

The town of Goliad sprang up around the mission, La Bahia (lä bä ē′ä).

In Spanish the letter "H" is always silent. Goliad was named in honor of Hidalgo. The silent letter is omitted, and the others rearranged.

Goliad is remembered as the place where Fannin and his men were massacred. There is a town in Goliad County named for Fannin. There are state parks both at Goliad and at Fannin.

GONZALES

The first battle of the Revolutionary War (when our nation won its independence) was fought at Lexington, Massachusetts. The first battle fought for the independence of Texas was at Gonzales. For this reason, Gonzales is often called the "Lexington of Texas."

There was a small cannon at Gonzales, used for protection against the Indians. The Mexican commander demanded that it be given to his army. The Texans put up a flag bearing the words, "Come and take it."

But they didn't take it!

It was at Gonzales that Sam Houston took command of the Texan army.

It was to Gonzales that Mrs. Dickinson fled to tell of the fall of the Alamo.

Today, in the center of the town square, stands a bronze statue by a famous Texan sculptor. The statue honors the brave men who took the first stand for Texan liberty.

COLUMBUS

Columbus is one of the oldest towns in the state. It is mentioned often in Texas History.

When Stephen F. Austin came to Texas, he found a few scattered families. Some of these were at Columbus. Some of The Old Three Hundred made their homes there.

Columbus was for a short time the capital of Texas.

Columbus is on the Colorado River, in a county named for the river. Colorado (cŏl′ō-rä′dō) is the Spanish word for red.

There is an interesting oak tree in this South Texas town. When the residents returned after the Battle of San Jacinto, the town lay in ruins. Santa Anna had burned their homes and other buildings. There was no other place to hold court, so it was held in the shade of this tree.

This giant tree still stands. A bronze tablet reminds us that here was held the first Court of the Republic of Texas.

CASTROVILLE

Thirty miles west of San Antonio is a small village. There is no other town in the state like it.

Almost a century ago, a group of people from Alsace (a borderland country between Germany and France), under the leadership of Henry Castro crossed the ocean to make their home in Texas.

Castro had been a soldier under Napoleon. So had others in the colony. They were tired of war and were looking for a home where they could live in peace, happy and free.

They built their homes and church and laid out their streets, like the villages of Alsace. Then they named the town Castroville, in honor of their leader.

These Alsatian settlers liked their new home. Their descendants still live there. They are good Texans. But, even today, Castroville seems like a little village of the Old World transplanted to our Texas hills.

Many tourists visit Castroville. Have you seen this interesting Texas town?

NEW BRAUNFELS

About a hundred years ago a group of people in Germany became dissatisfied with the government of their homeland. They wanted to make their home in a free country. There were several German settlements made in Texas. One of the most interesting was New Braunfels.

Prince Carl of Solms-Braunfels was sent to Texas to investigate. He reported that the land was fertile, the climate healthful, and the scenery beautiful.

Three ships filled with these colonists arrived at Galveston just before Christmas. They waited on the coast until spring, then started the hard trip inland. Most of the people walked or rode in oxwagons. But their leader, Prince Carl, traveled in a manner more becoming to a prince.

Wouldn't you like to have seen Prince Carl, dressed in his royal velvet robes and plumed hats, talking to the Indians?

The colonists lost their way and became discouraged. One of the Texas Rangers guided them to beautiful Comal Springs, the place which they were seeking. On this site they built their homes. Prince Carl named the town New Braunfels after the home he had left in Germany.

SAN ANGELO

San Angelo was laid out soon after the War between the States. Its founder named it the "City of the Angel" for his sister-in-law, a nun in San Antonio.

The surrounding country was, and is, ranch country. From its beginning, San Angelo was the cowboys' town. Wide sombreros, chaps, spurs, and Mexican costumes were seen on its streets daily. "Shootings" were not uncommon.

Today San Angelo is a beautiful, modern

city. But it has assembled reminders of these story-book days in the West Texas Museum.

BASTROP

Both the town and the county of Bastrop are named for Baron de Bastrop (bäs trō′). At the time Moses Austin came to San Antonio seeking permission to bring colonists, he was an alcalde. It was through his influence with the governor that Austin obtained this original land grant for his colonists.

Bastrop served Texas in many ways. You will read more about him in Texas History.

QUANAH

In an earlier chapter you read the story of Cynthia Ann Parker. Her oldest son, Quanah, became the chief of his tribe.

The town of Quanah, located near where his mother was rescued by the Texas Rangers, is named for this Indian Chief.

BANDERA

Not far from San Antonio is an interesting town, Bandera. Bandera is the Spanish word for *flag.* This is the story of how it got its name.

There was trouble between the Apache and Comanche Indians about the boundaries of their hunting grounds. Priests from San Antonio went out to attempt to make a treaty between the tribes. Bandera Pass, a natural pass through the Guadalupe (gwä dä lo͞o′pā) Mountains, was made the boundary. A flag upon the mountain was the sign of the treaty.

Bandera was settled by the Mormons almost a century ago. Later a Polish colony was established there.

Tourists to Bandera enjoy the Frontier Times Museum, which contains more than 15,000 items.

SAN PATRICIO

During the time when many groups of families were settling in Texas, two Irishmen obtained a land grant on the Nueces River. Their names were John McMullen and Patrick McGloin.

They named their townsite for the patron saint of Ireland, St. Patrick. But to the Spanish-speaking people of Texas it soon became known as San Patricio; and so it is called today.

San Patricio is in San Patricio County. McMullen County is also a part of the old Irish colony.

An interesting story is told of the Irish settlement.

About a year before the Battle of San Jacinto was fought, McMullen and McGloin asked the Mexican officials to come to talk over the problems of government. But the people of San Patricio invited them to a festival before the business meeting.

The Mexican company rode northward, dressed in their gayest costumes. The Irish, too, were dressed in their holiday attire as they rode out to meet them. The place where they met is called Banquete (bän kēt′) to this very day.

(Banquete is the Spanish word for *banquet.*)

What a festival they had! For three days and three moonlight nights they feasted and played their native games. The Mexican men said the Irish ladies were wonderful cooks. Soon the Irish could dance the Spanish fandango, and the Mexicans could do the Irish jig.

On the fourth day the leaders of the two parties held a serious conference. Soon everything was decided in a manner satisfactory to all.

You see, they had learned to know each other; and we usually like the people we know. They had become friends.

COLORADO CITY

Colorado City is in Mitchell County. The county is named for two Mitchell brothers of The Old Three Hundred in Austin's colony.

The town is on the banks of the Colorado River, and from it takes its name.

"Old-timers" still tell of many interesting things that happened here in the early days. Many times a Comanche or an Apache brave (the two tribes who were best known for daring feats on horseback) went riding across the mesquite-covered plains. The Comanches raided from the north, and the Apaches from the south and west. Sometimes these tribes even fought each other here.

A company of Texas Rangers was sent here in the early days of the town. About thirty men were encamped in what is now the center of Colorado City.

The years between 1870 and 1885 are called the Cattle Era of Texas. Colorado City was in the center of great ranches of these days. It was the first town in West Texas to be a railroad junction, so became a big shipping center. For many years mail for both Lubbock and Amarillo was sent to Colorado City by train and then taken overland by stagecoach.

In West Texas, all cattle trails led to Colorado City. Here the cowboys got their hot baths, haircuts, and swapped tall tales of ranch life.

Today Colorado City, the county seat of Mitchell County, is a farming, ranch, and oil center.

BROWNSVILLE

Brownsville, in the Magic Valley, is the most southern city in the United States. It was named for a fort established there. Fort Brown is an active military camp today.

Brownsville is in Cameron County. This county is named for Ewen Cameron, a Scotchman who came to Texas one year after the Battle of San Jacinto and became a hero in the Mier (myār) Expedition.

Many vegetables and much fruit are grown in the area around Brownsville. The weather never gets very cold. Flowers bloom the year round. Poinsettias grow in the yards, sometimes four or five feet tall. They are very beautiful as they blossom by almost every house at Christmas time.

Many Mexican-Texans live at Brownsville. The shops are gay with their handiwork.

An international airport, an international port of entry, and an international seaport are at Brownsville. These are all shared with our southern neighbor, Mexico.

UVALDE

Uvalde is in Uvalde County. Both the town and the county are named for Uvalde Canyon.

Many years ago the Apache Indians held the canyon as a stronghold, and from it made raids, robbing and killing. Ugalde, a Mexican governor, led a band of soldiers who pursued the Indians and defeated them. The canyon was named for him, though the spelling was changed through the years to Uvalde.

Many sheep and goats are raised near Uvalde, and much mohair is shipped from there. All about the town are hundreds of pecan trees. Uvalde honey is famous for its fine flavor. Have you tried it? Was it good?

Uvalde, Texas, is known throughout our nation as the home of John Nance Garner, a former Vice-President of the United States. On certain days, the Garner home is open to visitors. In a downtown hotel is Mr. Garner's gavel collection, and visitors to the town always wish to see this famous collection.

Have you seen it? If so, tell your classmates all about the Garner Gavel Collection.

SOMETHING YOU CAN DO

Locate every city and town mentioned in these stories.

How many of these towns have you visited?

Which town would you most like to see on your next vacation?

What is your favorite story of Texas towns?

What is the story of your town?

STORIES OF TEXAS COUNTIES

There are 254 counties in Texas, and the name of each one suggests a story. Had you thought of that?

Many people have had a share in the naming of the counties. Some are named for Indians, many by the Spanish explorers and priests, many more for Texas heroes, and a few for the geography of the country.

What are some of these stories of Texas counties?

ANGELINA COUNTY

Many, many years ago, when the first Spanish priests came to East Texas, they found a little Indian girl more eager than any of the others to learn all they taught. She stayed in the mission. Soon she could speak the Spanish language, read and write a little, and sew and cook. She under-

Camels went limping around over Texas.

stood what they taught her about the church, too. Soon everyone called her Angelina, or Little Angel. They called her native village Angelina's Village; and the stream that flowed by, Angelina's River.

When the missions in East Texas were abandoned, she went with the priests to a mission on the Rio Grande River. Here she stayed for about ten years. She acted as interpreter for many explorers and travelers. She became well known from Louisiana to Mexico City.

Angelina returned to her people and did missionary work among them. A few years later a mission was established for her village, no doubt upon her request.

Today we remember Angelina by calling a river and a county by her name.

ARCHER COUNTY

Archer County is named for Dr. Branch T. Archer, good friend of Stephen F. Austin. They and Wharton went to the United States to get help for Sam Houston's army.

Dr. Archer was a good doctor, a real friend to the pioneers, and a willing worker for Texas.

AUSTIN COUNTY

Austin County is named for Stephen F. Austin, the Father of Texas. When the railroads were built, they did not pass through San Felipe, the capital of Austin's colony. So today San Felipe is a small town. In the State Park in Austin County there stands a beautiful statue of Stephen Fuller Austin.

BAYLOR COUNTY

Baylor County, not far from the Red River, honors a pioneer family who worked for their community and fellowmen in the early days of Texas.

Dr. Henry W. Baylor was a surgeon in the Mexican War. He had two younger brothers who also came to Texas and won many friends. Their uncle, Hon. R. E. B. Baylor, was a well-loved friend of education for whom Baylor University was named.

BORDEN COUNTY

This county was named in honor of Gail Borden.

Is the name *Borden* a familiar word to you? Where did you see the word today?

Gail Borden was born in New York. As a young man he came to the South. He taught school in Mississippi and married there.

Then he came to Texas. Stephen F. Austin employed him to be chief surveyor in his colonies.

Mr. Borden was interested in inventions. He found a way to condense milk. Today condensed milk is found on the shelves of all grocery stores, and a large milk company bears the name of the man who patented this process.

The county seat is Gail.

BOWIE COUNTY

Bowie County is named for James Bowie, who died at the Alamo. The famous bowie knife was named for him.

When Travis saw that the siege of the Alamo was hopeless, with his sword he drew a line in the dirt floor. He gave all who wished to try to escape permission to do so. Then he told all who were willing to fight to the death with him to cross over the line. All the men crossed over except Bowie, who lay, very ill, on his cot. He asked two of his friends to lift his cot over the line.

They did. And today, visitors at the Alamo still ask to see the spot where the line was drawn and where Bowie's cot was lifted over.

BREWSTER COUNTY

When Henry Brewster was nineteen he heard of the fall of the Alamo. At once he packed his bag and left for Texas. He arrived just in time to take part in the Battle of San Jacinto.

At twenty, he began the practice of law. Everyone said young Brewster was a brilliant and thorough young lawyer. He served the state well in various offices.

Brewster County, the largest county in the state, is named for him.

CALDWELL

Caldwell was one of the signers of the Declaration of Texas Independence. He was a Texas Ranger. He was one of the commanders in the great fight with the Comanches at Plum Creek.

Caldwell County is named for him.

CASS COUNTY

Cass County is named for Lewis Cass, a senator from Michigan, who was a warm advocate of the annexation of Texas.

Cass County is on the Louisiana line.

CHEROKEE, COMANCHE, NACOGDOCHES, PECOS, AND WICHITA COUNTIES

Five counties of our state have been named for Indian tribes. They are Cherokee, Comanche, Nacogdoches, Pecos, and Wichita. Find these counties on the map.

CHILDRESS COUNTY

George C. Childress was born in Nashville, Tennessee. He came to Texas in 1832. He was a brilliant lawyer, so he was the chairman of the committee which prepared the Declaration of Independence. He is its author; so it is in his handwriting.

Have you seen a reproduction of the Declaration of Independence? Did you observe the handwriting of Childress?

Childress County, on the Red River, is named for him.

CROCKETT COUNTY

David Crockett's father was an Irishman. David was fun-loving and adventurous. He was a true frontiersman. Many stories are told about him.

Crockett County, in West Texas, is named for him. The town of Crockett, in Houston County, is also named for David Crockett.

DEAF SMITH

The name of this good old scout was Erastus Smith, but everybody called him Deaf Smith.

Have you seen the picture painted by Huddle? Sam Houston is lying under the live oak tree, talking to Santa Anna. Deaf Smith has his hand cupped to his ear, trying to hear what they are saying.

After the Battle of San Jacinto, Deaf Smith lived at Richmond. We may be sure that he, Mrs. Long, the Mother of Texas, and Mr. Lamar, the Father of Education in Texas, all knew each other well.

DENTON COUNTY

Denton County is named for a minister, John B. Denton. As was customary in those days, he had to support himself and family by other work. He studied law, and became a successful lawyer. While leading an Indian raid, he was killed by a barbed arrow.

ELLIS COUNTY

Richard Ellis, a lawyer and a large-scale cotton farmer, was elected president of the Convention at Washington-on-the-Brazos, March 2, 1836. Ellis County, one of the largest cotton-producing counties, is named for him.

HARRIS COUNTY

Harris County is named for John R. Harris, a friend of Moses Austin back in Missouri. He was granted land by the Mexican government. His townsite was named Harrisburg, and is now a part of Houston.

HENDERSON COUNTY

Henderson County is named for J. P. Henderson, the first governor of the state. He was a lawyer, and was born in North Carolina.

The great trees of this county are sold for lumber. Many vegetables are shipped from this county, too.

HILL COUNTY

Hill County is named for Dr. George W. Hill from Tennessee. He was a graduate of the same college that Stephen F. Austin attended. He came to Texas when he was only twenty-three years old. He accepted several appointments from the government, being Indian Agent and also Secretary of War. During all this time he kept up his medical practice. He was dearly loved by the people he served, who named this county for him while he was yet living.

JEFF DAVIS COUNTY

Jeff Davis County is named for Jefferson Davis, President of the Southern Confederacy.

Jeff Davis was an army man, a graduate of West Point Military Academy.

After the Mexican War several United States military forts were built in Texas.

Jefferson Davis was Secretary of War. He had been in Texas. He knew about the difficulty of transportation, for railroads had not yet been built. He knew about the scarcity of water. How would you like to haul drinking water for 2,000 horses?

"I know just the thing," said Davis. "We can use camels. When we come to a river they can get a good, long drink. Then they won't need any more water for at least five days. Camels are fast, so can get away from attacking Indians.

"Yes, that is the very thing to do. We shall get the camels at once."

And they did.

We know that at least eighty camels and twelve Arab drivers were brought into the state. They were sent to several forts, though most of them were sent to the fort near Bandera. Later many of them were taken to Fort Davis, in Jeff Davis County.

But there was one thing the Secretary of War forgot. A camel in his native desert country walks on deep, soft sand. The land in Texas, especially in mountainous regions where the forts were, is hard and rocky. The poor camels' feet became so sore they could hardly walk. It must have made a funny sight—all those camels limping around over Texas.

It didn't take long for everybody to know that the whole idea was a grand mistake.

The camels were sold, some to zoos and some to circuses. Some escaped from the forts, and became wild. For years afterward many strange stories were told about these camels living in the woods or hills. Just imagine how surprised you would be to come suddenly upon a camel on a walk through the woods. Would your family believe you, or do you think they might think you were just a little crazy?

Some of those who saw the camels in those days could hardly make the people believe that they were telling the truth.

Fort Davis was established in 1854. The soldiers were needed to protect settlers and travelers from the Comanches and Apaches. The old fort has been closed long ago, but the buildings still stand.

When the county was organized, like the fort and the town that had grown up around it, it was named for Jeff Davis.

JEFFERSON COUNTY

Jefferson County is named for Thomas Jefferson, author of the American Declaration of Independence and one of the presidents of the United States. He never came to Texas. He died about the time that many families were coming to Texas from the United States. The colonists settling here wished to honor this good American by naming their county in his honor.

The town of Jefferson, in Marion County, is also named for Thomas Jefferson. This town is on Cypress River, a tributary to the Red River. It had excellent water transportation, and at one time was one of the largest and most prosperous towns in the state. But when the railroads were built, Jefferson was not the shipping center it had been.

Jefferson, in East Texas, is a modern city today but visitors still enjoy seeing its beautiful homes and old buildings which remind us of the days when the town—and the state—were young.

KARNES COUNTY

Karnes County is named for Henry W. Karnes.

Henry Karnes was a scout under General Sam Houston. He was also a Texas Ranger.

Karnes was redheaded. Once he was captured by the Indians. They demanded to know how he dyed his hair. When he told them his hair just grew that way, they refused to believe him.

They took him to the river and nearly drowned him trying to wash the red from his hair.

Afterwards, Karnes would laugh when he told this story. But he said it wasn't at all funny to him the day it happened!

KENDALL COUNTY

Kendall County is named for a newspaper reporter.

George W. Kendall, born in New Hampshire, had a newspaper in New Orleans. It was a new and very small newspaper.

Kendall heard of the Santa Fe Expedition.

He told his partner of his plan.

"I'll join the expedition. Then I can write interesting, first-hand accounts. That should increase the circulation of the paper."

He was right. The articles in the paper were most interesting. He was taken prisoner, along with the Texans. The Santa Fe stories lasted about two years. And by that time his newspaper had become the largest in the Southwest.

Kendall decided to live in Texas. He bought a large tract of land in what is now Kendall County, and lived there the rest of his life.

LAMAR COUNTY

Mirabeau B. Lamar was born in Georgia, of French parents. He fought in the Battle of San Jacinto. He was the second President of the Republic of Texas. Because he laid the early plans for free public schools, he is called the Father of Education in Texas.

The county seat of Lamar County is Paris. Why do you think that name was chosen for the town?

LEE COUNTY

Lee County is named for Robert E. Lee. He is one of the great men of our country. You will read more about him in American history.

LEON COUNTY

Leon County was named for Martin de Leon, a Mexican empresario. An empresario, you remember, was one who had permission from the government to settle a stated number of families here. Austin was an empresario (ām prā sä′-ryō).

LUBBOCK

There were two of the Lubbock brothers who came to Texas in the early days. They were from South Carolina. F. R. Lubbock became governor of the state. Thomas Lubbock fought in several battles. Once he was captured and carried to Mexico, but escaped by jumping from a balcony.

Lubbock County is named for the Lubbock brothers.

MAVERICK COUNTY

Samuel Maverick was present that cold day at Washington-on-the-Brazos. He signed the Declaration to make Texas free.

He was a lawyer who was given cattle in payment for a debt. He was so busy with his law practice and real estate business that he did not look after the cattle very well. They grew fat on the range, but many of them were unbranded. The word *maverick* has come to mean unbranded calves.

Find the county named for Maverick on the map. What country lies just across the river?

McLENNAN COUNTY

Neil McLennan was born in Scotland. He came to Texas, with his family, a year before the Battle of San Jacinto. He first settled near the Gulf Coast. One day he and the Texas Ranger, Erath, were traveling together when they came to the Valley of the Bosque (bŏs′kē) River. McLennan thought he had never seen such beautiful scenery or such fertile land. He at once filed on land there, and moved his family to their new home. McLennan County is named for this Scottish pioneer.

MENARD COUNTY

Michael Menard was a French-Canadian. He came to Texas, three years before the Battle of San Jacinto, to trade with the Indians. He signed the Declaration of Independence. He was the founder of the city of Galveston.

Menard, the county seat of the county, is also named for this tall, pleasant Frenchman.

MILAM COUNTY

Milam County is named for Ben Milam from Kentucky.

Early in the war for Texan independence, he

asked a question that has come down to us as a common saying.

The Texan troops were just outside San Antonio, which was held by the Mexicans. The Texans hesitated to make the attack, since they were outnumbered four to one.

Ben Milam stepped out in front, waved his battered hat, and cried:

"Who will go with old Ben Milam?"

With a shout the men rushed forward. San Antonio was taken. Two men were killed, and one of them was brave Ben Milam.

NOLAN COUNTY

Nolan was the first filibuster (fĭl′ĭ bŭs′ter) in Texas. As the word is used in Texas History, filibuster means one who came into the country "on his own hook."

Nolan was a young Irishman, probably not more than twenty-two years old. He came into Texas to capture mustangs (mŭs′tăngs), which he sold for a good sum in Natchez or Louisiana. He made a map of Texas.

There was a misunderstanding about Nolan's right to enter Texas. He was killed in a battle near Waco.

We remember this gay young adventurer by naming a county for him.

PANOLA

Panola (pă nō′lȧ) is an Indian word meaning "cotton." Texas produces more cotton than any other state in the United States, so it is fitting that we should have a county named for "King Cotton."

ROBERTSON COUNTY

Robertson County is named for Sterling G. Robertson, another empresario. At one time this county contained all of eight counties and parts of others.

Sterling Robertson was from Tennessee. George C. Childress, author of the Texas Declaration of Independence, was his nephew.

ROCKWALL COUNTY

Rockwall County is the smallest county in the state. It is named for a rock wall which shows on the surfacc in many places. In years past much more of the wall showed above the ground. At one time people paid admission to see this unusual work of nature.

SAN JACINTO

San Jacinto County is named for the Battle of San Jacinto. It was not possible to name a county for each man who took part, but San Jacinto County is in honor of them all.

This county is in the Pine Belt. It lies within Sam Houston National Forest.

SHACKLEFORD COUNTY

Shackleford County, in West Texas, is named for Dr. John Shackleford. His nickname was Jack, so he is sometimes called Dr. Jack Shackleford.

He was spared at Goliad massacre because the enemy wanted him to treat their wounded soldiers. Although his own life was safe, he was far from happy. His own son, two nephews, and many friends were shot down.

Today many Herefords are grown on the ranches of Shackleford County.

SHERMAN COUNTY

This county was named for General Sidney Sherman. He was born in far-away Massachusetts. His forefather fought with George Washington to help win American independence.

General Sherman heard the pleas of Austin, Archer, and Wharton. Then he organized and equipped a company of fifty men and promptly left for Texas. At San Jacinto he helped to win Texan independence.

The first railroad in our state was built from Richmond to Harrisburg. Sherman went back to Boston and interested wealthy men in developing this new country. We remember Sherman today as the man who caused the first railroad to be built in Texas.

TRAVIS COUNTY

The family of William B. Travis were pioneers in South Carolina. The town, Travis, in that state is named for them.

Travis was a well educated man. He was a schoolteacher. Later he studied law, and practiced law at Anahuac (ä nä wäk′).

William B. Travis will always be remembered

as the brave young commander of the Alamo. Travis County is named for him.

Austin, the capital of the state, is in Travis County.

TYLER AND POLK COUNTIES

These counties are named for the presidents of the United States when Texas was annexed. The resolution was signed while Tyler was in office. Texas was officially admitted to the Union during Polk's term.

These counties adjoin each other in East Texas. Both counties have lumbering and agriculture.

WASHINGTON COUNTY

Washington County is named for George Washington, the Father of Our Country. His name is on every state map in the United States.

Washington-on-the-Brazos, where the Declaration of Independence was signed, is in this county. It is a state park now.

WILSON COUNTY

James C. Wilson was born in England. He was a minister, educated in the best schools on the British Isles. He was a member of the Mier (myār) Expedition and was held a prisoner in Mexico City.

Many peanuts are grown in Wilson County. Find it on the map.

ZAVALA COUNTY

Lorenzo de Zavala was born of Spanish parents in Mexico. He was educated in Spain. When Mexico won its independence from Spain, they had to have a constitution. Zavala helped to write it, and was its first signer.

When they were young men, Zavala was a friend of Santa Anna. But when Santa Anna made himself a dictator, Zavala would not accept a place in his government. He came to Texas and helped to win her freedom from Mexico. He was one of the signers of the Declaration of Texas Independence.

Zavala County is named for this freedom-loving Spanish-Mexican.

YOUNG ARTISTS AND YOUNG WRITERS

Now, wouldn't you like to write the history of your county?

If it is mentioned in this book, there are many other facts you can add to your story. If your county is not included here, you can write your own book about it. This is how you can do it.

First, you must do the research. That means to find out all the facts you possibly can.

You must read all the books that have been written about your county. You will get some help from *Texas Almanac* and *History and Geography of Texas,* by Fulmore; Steck Company, Austin.

Then you must go to see some old people who lived in your county many years ago. They will tell you all they remember, and you will write it down.

Then you will learn of others who once lived in your county, but who have moved away. You will write letters to them.

Some people will be kind enough to let you read old newspaper clippings, old letters, and see old pictures in their scrapbooks.

Now you will be ready to begin your writing. Make your story as alive and interesting as you can. Put in the exact words of the speaker as often as you can. Give exact details, as the color of a person's eyes or the time of year.

When your story is finished, read it aloud. Did it make you feel as though you were really there, taking part in what happened?

Rewrite the parts you and your teacher think you can make better.

Perhaps your class will want to write the history of your county as a group activity. If so, make your plans together and choose a committee to prepare each part.

Best Wishes, Young Writers!

THE AUTHOR

Oh! You want to make an illustration? What fun! Well, this is how to go about it.

Read the story, trying to see pictures as you do so. Make a list of the parts that would be good to illustrate. Select the one that brings out the most important point. Make a quick sketch of the way you saw the picture. If you are not sure of the costumes, the surroundings, or the customs, find books which will give you correct information. Do not copy pictures but study them to get the facts you need. Use the facts in making your picture correct. Find actual objects and make drawings of them whenever you can.

If there are people in your picture, you may have difficulty getting them drawn in the position you desire. You can always find people who will be glad to pose for you. This is the way to be independent of other artists' drawings. It is as dishonest to copy someone's drawing as it is to copy words during a spelling test—unless you do it to learn how and do not show it as your own work.

Be sure to make the main idea large enough to be seen easily. It is better not to bother with details that do not help to illustrate your point.

Now, let's get busy drawing!

THE ARTIST

SYMBOLS OF TEXAS

STATE FLAG

The Lone Star Flag that we know today as the state flag was first the flag of the Republic of Texas. It was designed by Dr. Charles B. Stewart and was adopted in 1839.

When Texas became a state in the United States, the Lone Star Flag became the state flag.

The Texas Star in Old Glory is the twenty-eighth star. You can easily find it. It is the fourth star in the fourth row.

SALUTE TO THE TEXAS FLAG

In 1933 the legislature adopted the following pledge to the Texas flag:

Honor the Texas Flag,
I pledge allegiance to thee—
Texas, one and indivisible.

In giving the pledge, one should place the right hand on the heart and look directly at the flag, just as one salutes the national flag.

THE STATE SEAL

The state seal was adopted in 1836, before the flag was adopted. Like the flag, it was first the official emblem of the Republic. The seal is a five-pointed star, encircled by a wreath of olive and live oak branches.

THE STATE FLOWER

The bluebonnet is the state flower. It was adopted in 1901. The bluebonnet and certain other wild flowers are protected by law.

Never pick bluebonnets, dogwood, redbud, Indian paint brush, or bluebells along the state highway. They can be taken from private property only with the permission of the owner of the land.

THE STATE BIRD

The mockingbird is the state bird, adopted in 1927. He proclaims happiness and good will in a friendly, cheerful manner.

The pecan is our state tree.

THE STATE TREE

The pecan is our state tree. It was adopted in 1919. Many people believe that the pecan was selected because of James Stephen Hogg's love for this tree.

THE STATE SONG

The state song is "Texas, Our Texas." It was adopted in 1929.

THE STATE MOTTO

The motto of the state of Texas is "Friendship." It was adopted in 1930. The Indian word *Tejas* means friends.

The Spaniards changed the spelling, making the middle letter *x* rather than *j*. In this way the word *Texas* was formed.

SOMETHING YOU CAN DO

At other places in the book, other symbols are illustrated. Find them.

Make a scrapbook about the Symbols of Texas.

THE BLUEBONNET

The bluebonnet grows in almost all parts of the state except the far West and the Rio Grande Valley. It was officially made the state flower in 1901.

Mexican Texans call the bluebonnet "El Conejo" because they think the white top resembles the tail of the cottontail rabbit.

The bluebonnet is often called buffalo clover. This is an appropriate name, for it was a favorite food of the buffaloes. In sections where bluebonnets grew, there would be found herds of bison. Since the buffalo provided food, clothing, and shelter for the Indians, buffalo clover was a plant highly esteemed by the Indians.

There is a saying that the bluebonnet is a home-loving plant, and never crosses the state line of Texas.

There are many legends of the bluebonnet. Many people believe that the one of the unselfish little Indian maiden is the most beautiful of them all.

Her dearest treasure was her doll.

LEGEND OF THE TEXAS BLUEBONNET
(Poem)

Wild and wayward were the children,
Of the younger days of Tejas.
Thus the Great White Spirit taught them,
Taught his careless, thankless children
To obey and sacrifice.

Sent a long and frozen Winter,
When the woodland streams were ice bound,
And the prairies were forsaken
By the roving buffalo.
And the Redmen came in sorrow
While the wild wind whistled round them;
Cried aloud to the Great Spirit,
Begging that he melt the rivers,
Send the wild grass to the prairies,
Calling back the buffalo.

As they prayed, a mighty thunder
Rocked the prairies and the heavens;
And the voice, Great Spirit, answered,
"Give to me a sacrifice.
Bring to me your dearest treasure!
Lay it down upon the embers;
Cast the ashes to the Four Winds.
Then the earth shall bloom again."

But the Indians sat in silence,
For no man could bring his dearest.

Softly came a little maiden,
Hugging to her breast a treasure,
While her tears fell on the feathers
Of the doll she loved and fondled.
White its dress was—made of doeskin,
Blue its feathers from the bluejay,
And she laid it on the embers.

Came the voice of the Great Spirit,
"See, the fields are blue with clover.
Rise, Ye Redmen. It is Spring!
All your tribe shall be forgiven
Through the sacrifice of one."

And the Indians rose and thanked Him
In a dance of joy and praise.

—EMMA PETTEY

LEGEND OF THE TEXAS BLUEBONNET

(Story)

Long, long ago the Tejas Indians lived in our land. They were very happy here, hunting and fishing all the sunny day. The Indian braves hunted the buffaloes, and then there was food for all.

There came a long, cold winter. The buffaloes grew thin, and the Indians became hungry. They said, "How glad we shall be when spring comes!"

But when spring came it rained so long and so hard that it washed the young buffalo clover up by the roots. The Indians were very sad, for they were very hungry.

At last the rains stopped, and the Indians thought that at last everything would be all right. But it became so hot and so dry that the buffalo clover became parched and brown.

The Indian Chief called a meeting. When the Indians sat down on the ground, the chief stood up and spoke to them. He said, "The Great Spirit has spoken to me. Some one here must give up his dearest treasure."

Every person there thought of the thing he loved best in all the world. A man thought of his little boy. He couldn't give him up. A woman thought of her little girl. She couldn't give her up. One by one the Indians silently went away.

The Indian Chief's little girl was too small to go to the meeting but she was standing nearby and had heard all that her father said. Her dearest treasure was her doll—so beautiful in its white deerskin dress. In its hair were bright blue feathers from the bluejay. She thought of how hungry her people were—but she hugged her doll closer than ever.

During the night the little girl waked and decided what she should do. She walked out into the moonlight, and laid down the doll she loved so dearly as a gift to the Great Spirit.

Suddenly a wonderful thing happened! The sun was just coming up over the eastern hills. The earth became green with the leaves of the buffalo clover. And there were blue flowers—

so blue it looked as if a patch of sky had fallen!

The kind and unselfish little Indian maiden had saved all her tribe.

And this is the legend of the Texas bluebonnet.

STORY TIME

Learn to tell the story, "Legend of the Texas Bluebonnet."

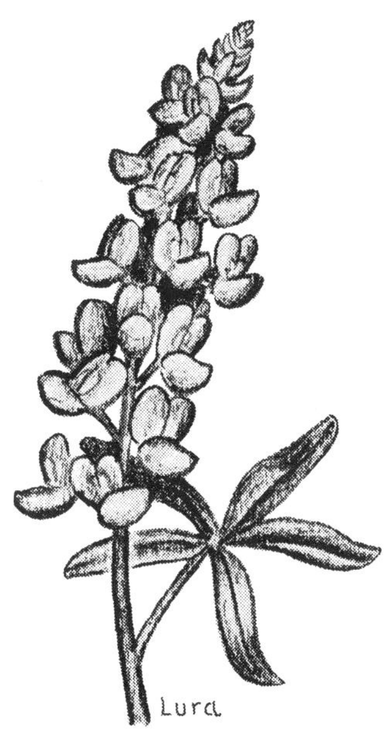

THE SQUIRE OF UVALDE

The year was 1851. Texas was a new state in the United States.

A covered wagon rumbled along the road from Tennessee to the crossing on the Red River at Jonesboro. The driver of the wagon was a beautiful woman with strong, brave features. She was a widow, Mrs. John Nance Garner, 2nd.

In the wagon were six children, three girls and three boys. The six-year-old boy, John Nance Garner, 3rd, was named for his father.

They reached the crossing on the Red River between Arkansas and Texas.

The children were all excited, especially young John Nance.

"Hey," he called, "the ferryman told me this was where Sam Houston crossed over into Texas."

"And David Crockett, too," said his brother, who had been doing a little exploring on his own.

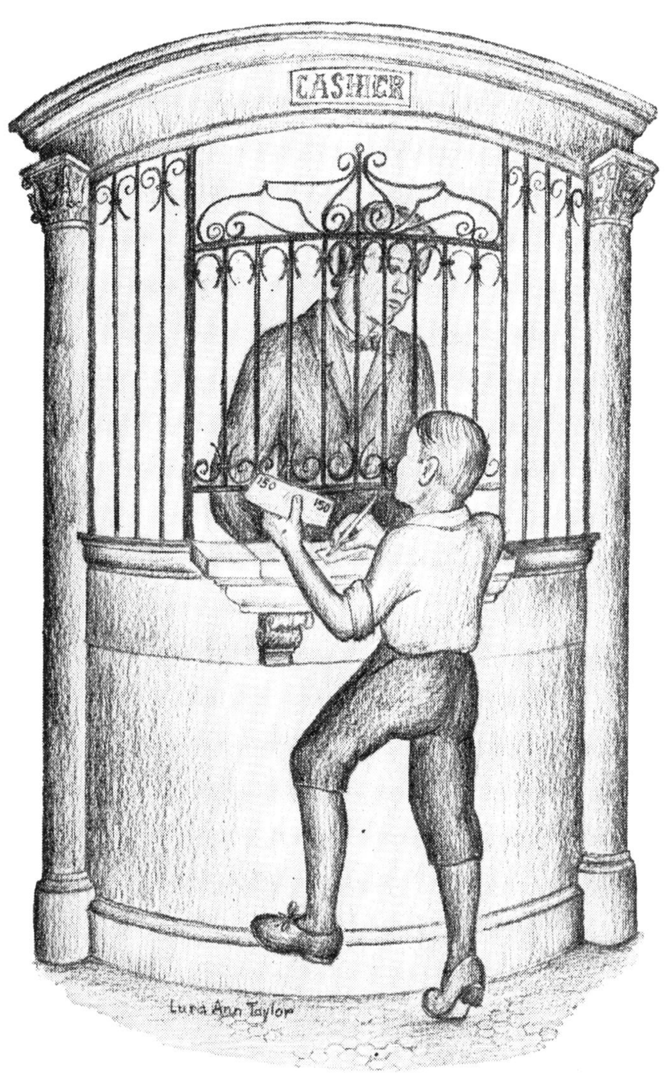

John banked the whole amount.

"Well, you boys needn't think you know everything," said Kitty, their sister. "Do you see that big tree at the bank? I've found out that is where the people tied up their canoes while they attended church services held in the shade of those large trees over there. All that was more than twenty-five years ago. They have built a church building now and roads are being built over the countryside."

The family settled in Red River County. Though Mrs. Garner had been reared in a well-to-do family, and as the young wife in the cultured Garner family had lived a sheltered life, she now did a woman's work and a man's work, too. By her hard work and good management, and with the help of all the children, the rich red soil of their farm provided a comfortable living and a steadily growing savings.

Then came the dark days of the Civil War. John Nance Garner, 3rd, became a cavalryman in the Confederate Army.

At the close of the war he rode sadly home again. Times were very hard in the South during the years just after the War between the States.

John Garner, 3rd, was twenty-one now,

strong and tall. He built himself a mud-chinked log cabin and married Sarah Guest, the prettiest girl at Blossom Prairie.

Their first child was born there on November 22, 1868. The baby was a boy and they named him for his father, John Nance Garner, 4th.

At the time that this baby was born in the Garner home, the man who was Vice-President of the United States was the only man ever to serve as both Speaker of the national House of Representatives and Vice-President of the United States.

In time, this child, John Nance Garner, 4th, became the only other man in America to be so honored.

Years went by. Times became better, and young John Garner's father became prosperous. He built the largest and most beautiful home in that part of the state. It was made from choice lumber, hauled in an oxwagon from Jefferson, Texas.

The home was noted for its hospitality. There were many visitors. Oftentimes the talk was of politics and government. The growing boy, John, heard talk of Richard Coke, Dick Hubbard, James A. Garfield, and others. The conversation of the older men interested the boy deeply.

Along came John's eighth birthday. One of his father's hired men wanted to give the boy a birthday present, but he was afraid John's father would not let him accept money as a gift. So he offered the boy five dollars if he would pick 100 pounds of cotton.

John picked 108 pounds, took the five dollars, and bought a motherless mule colt. Three years later he sold it for $150, and promptly banked the whole amount. From that day on there has never been a time when John Nance Garner did not have money in the bank. All through the years he has increased the amount until he now controls several banks and is one of the biggest money-lenders in the nation.

Even as a young boy, John knew he wanted book learning. Though his mother was busy looking after her six children—also three boys and three girls—she found time to teach her children the alphabet and other early lessons.

Aunt Kitty Garner had never married. She taught John to read, and write, and spell. She also had a shelf of good books and from these she read aloud to the little boy.

John's childhood years were pleasant. Besides their own six children, Mr. and Mrs. Garner reared seven more. The children worked and played together. There were swimming holes, and fishing streams, and a bobtailed dog named Rover.

Then John walked three miles to attend school in an unpainted schoolhouse. His teacher said he was the best pupil in the whole school.

When John was fifteen, he wanted to attend a school in Lamar County. This school had two very fine teachers, and some people said it was the best one in the state.

John still had the mule money and a little more.

"I am willing to work after school," he said. "I don't think I'll have to ask for help."

And he didn't.

The country was changing. A small town, Dallas, was growing rapidly since the building of the railroads. Water transportation was declining. Some said that Dallas might some day be even larger than Jefferson, but others laughed at such a foolish notion.

At the school in Lamar County, John played on the baseball team. He was the shortstop, and a good one, too.

When O. M. Roberts was a candidate for governor, he spoke at Paris. He made his campaign on two points, better schools and economical, "pay-as-you-go" government.

Garner later said that this speech, along with his father's teaching, influenced both his private and public financial management.

John Garner entered college but he became ill and returned home. He studied law in the office of a family friend. At twenty-one, he was admitted to the bar and set up practice in Clarksville, Texas.

For his health's sake, the doctor said he must go west. John Garner learned of an opening at Uvalde, and began to pack his bag.

He went to his parents to tell them good-by. He asked if they had any advice to give him.

"Only this, John," said his father. "Tell the truth and be a gentleman."

As the train traveled west from San Antonio, Mr. Garner noticed that the houses were far apart. This was a new country. Perhaps he could grow up with the country here as his father had done in Red River.

He reached Uvalde at night. As soon as the bank opened next morning, he went in and opened an account with $150. The signature he left at the bank was *Jno. N. Garner;* and that has remained his signature through life. Today he owns that bank and other banks in near-by towns.

From the bank, he walked to the law office. Before the day ended, a new sign had been put up: Clark, Fuller, & Garner.

He did well from the start. Not all his fees were paid in cash. But Garner was a good trader, so no matter how he was paid he not only got his money but also made a profit.

When he was twenty-five years old, Garner was elected county judge.

While serving in this office, he met and married Miss Mariette Rheiner, daughter of a Swiss immigrant.

Miss Rheiner was a graduate of a fashionable boarding school in Tennessee. She was lonely on her father's big ranch, so announced that she was going to take a course in a business school in San Antonio. Such a thing for a girl of means was unheard of in those days. But this intelligent girl had a mind of her own. This business course served her in good stead. Even when her husband was Vice-President of the United States, she was his secretary.

In September, 1896, their only child was born. The baby was a boy, and was named Tully Fuller for Mr. Garner's law partner.

Mr. and Mrs. Garner built a home. Garner had a good law library and was collecting a home library that was to make him one of the best-read men in the nation. He was investing in bank stock and real estate. He was doing well; but he had made up his mind to serve his state in the national Congress.

Garner served first in the state legislature. Like Stephen F. Austin, he is not a large man. He was thirty-three when he walked into the new capitol at Austin, but he looked very much like a boy.

November 9, 1903, John Nance Garner walked into the National Capitol and took a seat in the House of Representatives.

He was to remain in Washington thirty-eight years. Again and again he was re-elected. John Nance Garner was for many years Speaker of the House and, as Vice-President, he was Speaker of the Senate.

Garner was known in Washington as one who did not waste words and a man who could get things done. The following are some of his well-known statements:

"When I say anything I mean it."

"Nobody can do everything he wants to."

"I hear you will stand without hitching. I am glad of that. Out in my country a horse isn't worth much unless he will do that."

Mr. and Mrs. Garner lived a simple life in Washington just as they had done in Uvalde.

He got up at 6:00 A.M., ate a hearty breakfast, and was in his office at 7:30 every morning. Nine o'clock was his usual bedtime.

As Speaker of the House, Garner was entitled to an official car; but he did not take it.

"It doesn't take an automobile to make the office dignified. I'll lend the dignity," he said.

But Garner was also setting an example of government economy. Like Benjamin Franklin, he believes in thrift and abhors waste.

All through the years Mr. Garner's favorite recreation was an occasional fishing trip with Ross Brumfield, a garage owner at Uvalde. Once after one of these trips some friends from Washington called on him.

"You look like the original red-white-and-blue candidate," one said. "Red face, white hair, and blue eyes."

During all the years in Washington, Mr. Garner made frequent trips to the Washington Zoo.

"Some people talk too much. The animals don't," he said.

On January 20, 1941, Mr. Garner's long career in the national capital ended. He and Mrs. Garner had enjoyed the years in Washington, but they were glad to come back to their own home and old friends in Uvalde.

Garner owns great tracts of land. In England, the nobles owning much land are called squires. John Nance Garner is sometimes called the "Squire of Uvalde."

Mr. Garner believes that a family who own their own home make better citizens. He is now building homes and selling them on terms. Sometimes, someone laughingly says, "This is the house that Jack built."

Over and over again Mr. Garner has said that getting along with people is something that every person must learn to do. Without learning this important lesson one can hardly expect to have a successful and happy life.

The Garner home in Uvalde is set among giant oak and pecan trees. The lawn covers eight acres and is thickly carpeted with San Augustine grass.

The Garner lawn is a bird sanctuary. Mr. Garner enjoys watching the many kinds of birds which come. He is a great lover of animals, too.

Nearby lives his son, Tully, and wife. His granddaughter, Genevieve, is married and has two small sons, John Garner Currie and Tully Robert Currie.

Mr. Garner enjoys these great-grandsons very much. He has great faith in the future of America, for he believes that these boys and other young Americans will grow up to become men and women who will keep our government sound and wise and fair.

John Nance Garner has been called "Cactus Jack." President Roosevelt called him "Mr. Commonsense." In Uvalde he is called simply Mr. Garner or Judge Garner. But in Texas outside his home town he is called the "Squire of Uvalde."

Once Garner, Will Rogers, and other friends made a tour of the states together. Will Rogers said of him, "You know, Garner is quite a man."

All Texas agrees with Will Rogers.

The "Squire of Uvalde" is quite a man.

QUESTIONS FOR YOUNG CITIZENS

Garner was interested in good government. So was James S. Hogg, and many, many others. Are you?

Is the responsibility of good government on a few people or all people?

Is it the duty of every good citizen to vote?

Who is the President of the United States today?

Who is the Vice-President?

Who is the Governor of Texas?

THE TEJAS HAD THE RIGHT IDEA

"The Tejas had the right idea. They believed in peace, in friendship between men and nations. And the Texans who walk their ground today have that same idea.

"In Texas, in the United States, in the Americas, and across the seas, the spirit of the Tejas must go on—the spirit of the friendly Indians who gave a great name to a great state." *

Yes, the Tejas had the right idea. It is best to be friendly. It is right to respect the point of view and the work of other people.

Texas has been made by people from many lands.

The Indians lived here first. Our state was named for the friendly tribes, not for those who fought and killed.

* *Texas the Land of the Tejas*—Siddie Joe Johnson, copyright Random House Inc., New York, N. Y.

Then came the Spanish priests, building missions here. Within the mission would be Indians from several tribes. They came to know and like each other. We may be very sure that these mission Indians tried to stop quarreling and fighting between the tribes.

Next came the colonists, the people who had come to make their homes here. They came by covered wagon and by boat, from many states and many countries.

Many came from the nearby southern states, bringing with them negroes to till the cotton fields and help in many other ways.

But every state was the former home of some of these pioneers.

They came from lands across the sea.

Lorenzo de Zavala was born in Mexico of Spanish parents and was educated in Spain.

George B. Erath, famous Texas Ranger, was born in Austria.

Niel McLennan, for whom McLennan County was named, came from Scotland.

Baron de Bastrop was from Holland, schooled in Prussia, and in the employ of Spain.

Stephen F. Austin, the Father of Texas, was a southern gentleman, the son of a Connecticut Yankee.

Texas has been made great by people from many lands.

Among those who were slain at the Alamo was a Jew.

With Houston at San Jacinto were soldiers from many states and at least ten foreign countries. A fifer from Bavaria led the music. A doctor from Ireland treated Sam Houston's broken ankle.

Perhaps the only man in the Battle of San Jacinto born in Texas was Antonio Navarro. He was born in San Antonio. His father was from the Isle of Corsica.

A few years ago in a classroom in Texas the pupils were studying Texas History. They were reading about the Battle of San Jacinto.

A little boy said, "Stephen F. Austin helped to win the victory even though he wasn't there. Austin is a distant kinsman of mine."

And a little girl answered, "I have recently moved to Texas. My people are from Ohio. My forefathers helped to send the Twin Sisters."

All the boys and girls thought her forefathers, far away in Ohio, had helped to win the victory, too. Do you agree that they were right?

Yes, Texas has been made great by people from many lands.

At first they dressed differently and spoke different languages. Their ideas were very different about the food they ate, about what one should study in school, about ways of worship.

Then because most of the people were friendly and fair, in most communities there came to be a common understanding.

That means that Juan might say, "I like the clothes you wear better than mine. I think I, too, shall wear your kind of clothes."

And John will smile and answer, "Thank you. I like your music and dances. Will you teach me to sing one of your songs?"

To be a Texan does mean something a little different. We like to think it means something rather special.

Is it something to brag about? Perhaps a little, just in fun. But not really. No, not ever. Only cowards and egoists brag.

A good Texan is proud of the brave deeds and rich drama of the past. He may live in a house of Spanish architecture, near a river named by the French, in a country named for the Irish, and his own forefathers might have come to Texas from Tennessee or Maine.

A good Texan is proud of the dream of the future. And he works to make that dream come true.

Everybody is agreed that there should be more

friendliness and fairness within the nation and the world. We must begin at home. Let us keep the spirit of the Tejas in our state, our country, and the world.

The Tejas had the right idea!

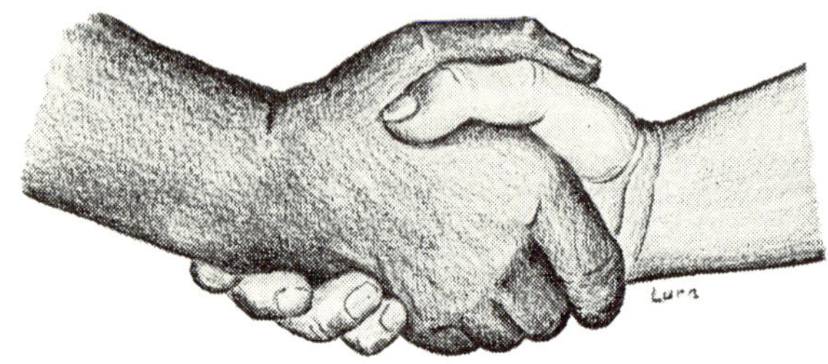

REMEMBER THIS, YOUNG TEXAN

The forefathers of Texas were strong and brave, and had great dreams for the future. All the work of building a state has not yet been done. You can help to build a still greater Texas.

Cabeza de Vaca was the first white man to tread on Texas soil. He was a Spaniard, and because of his explorations Spain claimed Texas.

The second flag to wave over Texas was the French flag. The Frenchman, La Salle, set it above his fort on Matagorda Bay.

The Spanish established missions in Texas. The most beautiful one is Mission San Jose at San Antonio. It is called the Queen of the Missions.

Stephen F. Austin is called the Father of Texas.

Mrs. Jane Long is called the Mother of Texas.

Sam Houston was the Commander-in-Chief of the Texan Army at San Jacinto.

Texas is the only state to ever have State Rangers. They were organized more than a hundred years ago.

Texas is the only state to ever have a navy.

The San Jacinto Battlefield is a state park. It is not far from Houston, on the road to Galveston.

A little girl, Cynthia Ann Parker, was captured by the Comanches one month after the Battle of San Jacinto. She grew up with the Indians and married the Indian Chief.

Even in the early days, the people here attended church services. Before the church buildings were erected, services were held out-of-doors or in someone's home.

Mr. Thomas Jefferson Pilgrim was a pioneer teacher in Texas. He taught here for almost fifty years. He established the first Sunday School in the state.

A pioneer doctor, Dr. Charles B. Stewart, designed the lone star flag.

James S. Hogg was one of the greatest governors Texas ever had. He was the first governor that had been born in Texas.

The name of every town and county has an interesting story.

There are 254 counties in Texas.

The bluebonnet is the state flower.

Do you know the other symbols of your state?

John Nance Garner of Uvalde is the only man

from Texas ever to be Vice-President of the United States.

The Tejas had the right idea. It is best to be friendly and fair. If you believe as the Tejas did, you will enjoy the film, *House I Live In;* Young America; 1946; 10 minutes; Sound. This film may be secured from the State Film Library or perhaps from your local film library.

NOW TELL ME TRUE

Find the best answer, the part that makes the sentence correct and true.

1. Pioneer settlers in Texas were
   - always lonely
   - always frightened
   - usually busy and happy

2. We honor certain men in history because
   - they did great deeds
   - they lived a long time ago
   - they are in the book

3. If I made a trip to Austin, I should want most of all
   - to go to a movie
   - to see the State Capitol
   - to see the shops and stores

4. History
   - is all in the book

was all made by our forefathers
is still being made

5. All the brave and important tasks in Texas
were done by our forefathers
were left undone
have not all been done, and I can help do them

DICTIONARY

Learn the meaning of these words. They have been used in these stories. Now use them in sentences of your own.

abhors (ăb hors′) To dislike very much; to detest.
abolish (ȧ bŏl′ish) To do away with.
abundant (ȧ bŭn′dănt) More than enough.
academy (ȧ kăd′ĕ mĭ) A school.
admiration (ăd′mĭ rā′shŭn) Honor; respect; approval.
alcalde (äl käl′dā; in Texas usually called ăl căl′dĕ) Spanish word for ruler of a town; mayor.
amazed (ȧ māzed′) Very much surprised.
ash hopper (ăsh hŏp′per) A box-like container found in every pioneer home. Small amounts of water were poured over wood ashes. The fluid drained out was lye, and was mixed with fats to make soap.
benefit (bĕn′ē fĭt) Help.
coffee mill (kŏf′fĕ mĭl) A small mill for grinding

coffee beans. In pioneer days, the coffee was ground each day for breakfast; and this task was usually assigned to the children.

constant (kŏn′stănt) Unchanging; all the time.

cooperation (kō ŏp′er ā′shŭn) Working together.

cotton cards (cŏt′ŭn cards) An article for smoothing cotton by hand. Carded cotton is put in quilts and mattresses.

cuirass (kwē răs′) A piece of armor covering the body fom neck to waist; an iron or strong leather jacket.

courage (kur′ĭg) Bravery.

courier (kŏŏr′ĭ er) A messenger.

creche (krāsh) French word for Manger Scene.

cultured (kŭl′tûred) Well educated; having refined manners.

cunning (kŭn′ĭng) Clever.

defeat (dē fēt′) Failure; loss of a game or contest.

delirium (dē lĭr′ĭ ŭm) A temporary condition of the mind; "out of the head."

disposition (dĭs′pō zĭsh′ŭn) One's habit of mind and behavior; as, kind disposition or grouchy disposition.

distinguished (dĭs tĭng′gwĭsht) Better than average in ability; having excelled in deeds and services.

donate (dō′nāt) To give.

dwindle (dwĭn′dl) To become less.

efficient (ĕ fĭsh′ent) Capable; competent; doing one's work well.

egotistic (ē′gō tĭs′tĭk) Thinking and talking too much of oneself.

elaborate (ē lăb′ō rāt) Complete in every detail.
emergency (ē mer′gĕn sĭ) Something that demands attention at once.
engineer (ĕn′jĭ nēr′) A man skilled in the science of developing natural power and resources in ways that are useful to man. One who operates an engine, as the engineer of a train.
exaggeration (ĕg zăj′er ā′shŭn) Overstatement; enlargement of the facts.
exasperated (ĕg zăs′per āt ĕd) Annoyed; angered.
extinct (ĕks tĭngkt′) No longer living or active.
fertile (fur′tĭl) Rich; fruitful.
festival (fĕs′tĭ văl) A celebration; sometimes feasting and celebration.
flat iron (flăt ī′urn) Object heated at wood fires and used for ironing clothes.
flint (flĭnt) A very hard stone which strikes fire when rubbed together; used in pioneer homes instead of matches.
foresight (fōr′sīt) Knowing something before it happens; preparation for the future.
frontier (frŭn tēr′) The edge of a settled country; the unknown and unexplored.
gallantly (găl′ănt lȳ) With courage; with bravery.
gourd dipper (gōrd dĭp′per) A water dipper made from a gourd.
gracious (grā′shŭs) Attractive and kind in manner and character.
granary (grăn′ȧ rĭ) Storehouse for grain.
hospitality (hŏs′pĭ tăl′ĭ tȳ) Kindness and politeness to guests.

inherited (ĭn hĕr′ĭt ĕd) Received by birth from one's forefathers.
injustice (ĭn jŭs′tĭs) Without fairness; wrong.
interpreter (ĭn ter′prĕ ter) One who explains; one who can speak two languages to make conversation between persons speaking different languages understood.
investigate (ĭn vĕs′tĭ gāt) To examine; to look into.
irrigation (ĭr′ĭ gā′shŭn) The furnishing of a water supply by ditches to farmland.
lea (lē) Meadow.
legal (lē′găl) Lawful.
loom (lo͞om) A frame or machine for weaving cloth. Every pioneer home had a loom.
majority (mȧ jor′ĭ tў̆) More than half.
massacre (măs′ȧ ker) The killing of many people.
molten (mōl′tĕn) Melted.
munition (mū nĭsh′ŭn) War material.
native (nā′tĭv) Natural; belonging by right of birth.
observation (ŏb′zer vā′shŭn) That which is noticed or learned.
occupation (ŏk′ū pa′shŭn) One's business or work.
ochre (ō′ker) Also spelled ocher. A clay containing iron ore used as coloring in paint.
omen (ō′mĕn) A sign.
overwhelmingly (ō′ver whĕlm′ĭng lў̆) Completely; covered, as by a great wave.
peril (pĕr′ĭl) Danger.
permanent (pur′mȧ nent) Lasting; fixed.
plantation (plăn tā′shŭn) A large farm.

plaza (plä′zȧ or plăz′ȧ) A public square; a downtown park.

poultry (pōl′trĭ) Domestic birds that furnish meat or eggs for human food; as, chickens, turkeys, ducks, geese, etc.

preceded (prē sēd′ed) Went before; happened before.

prepared (prē pâred′) Ready.

pretend (prē tĕnd′) To make believe.

procession (prō sĕsh′ŭn) A formal parade, as a religious procession or a wedding procession.

protested (prō tĕst′ĕd) Objected to; stated one's disapproval.

provisional (prō vĭzh′ŭn ăl) Serving for a short time; not permanent.

prudence (prōō′dĕns) Wisdom; good judgment.

pursue (per sū′) To chase.

rampage (răm pāj′) Riotous or wild behavior.

recorded (rē kord′ĕd) Set down in writing or some other permanent record.

reluctantly (rē lŭk′tănt lȳ) Unwillingly.

resign (rē zīn′) To give up a position or office.

scalpel (skăl′pĕl) A small knife used by doctors.

scholarly (skŏl′er lȳ) Knowing a great deal about one or more subjects.

security (sē kū′rĭ tȳ) Freedom from fear; protection.

sedate (sē dāt′) Quiet; refined.

shoe last (shōō lăst) An iron last upon which shoes are put to be repaired. A shoe last was found in every pioneer home, for the father mended his family's shoes.

siesta (sĭ ĕs′tȧ) An afternoon nap.

slate and pencil (slāt and pĕn′sĭl) Used by school children instead of tablet and pencil.

spinning wheel (spĭn′nĭng whēl) Cotton or wool was spun into threads, from which cloth was woven. A spinning wheel was standard equipment in a pioneer home.

squire (skwīr) One who owns much land; a nobleman.

tale (tāl) A story.

toil (toil) Work.

transplanted (trăns plant′ed) Changed (a plant) from one place to another.

trundle bed (trŭn′d'l bed) A low bed that is moved on trundles, or little wheels, so that it can be pushed under a higher bed.

twilight (twī′līt) The dim light before sunrise or after sunset.

typical (tĭp′ĭ kăl) Like many others in a group.

unaccustomed (ŭn′ă kŭs′tŭmed) Not usual; unfamiliar.

unaware (ŭn′ȧ wâr) Not knowing.

unbuilded (ŭn bĭld′ĕd) Not built; unmade.

unique (ū nēk′) Unusual; different from others.

valiant (văl′yănt) Brave.

varied (vâr′ĭd) Of many kinds or sorts.

ventilation (vĕn′tĭ lā′shŭn) Movement of fresh air.

vision (vĭzh′ŭn) A picture created by the imagination.

Webster's Blue Back Speller. The most important textbook one hundred years ago.

INDEX